Packed with insightful suggestions and superb ideas for service opportunities all around us.

> Stephen R. Covey
> Author of *The 7 Habits of Highly Effective People*
> and *The 8th Habit: From Effectiveness to Greatness*

Terri Cannavo has created a wonderful resource for anyone that is in a service-related profession. It gives us a guide and reference for life's complexities that come across our paths in every walk of life.

> LuJean Tatton, president
> National Cosmetology Association of Utah

This book is a great resource for two types of people: those who want to provide service but simply don't know how, and those who have grand intentions, but can't muster up the energy to achieve their goals and end up doing nothing.

> Lynette Rasmussen, director
> Office of Work and Family Life
> Department of Workforce Services
> Salt Lake City, Utah

In a Hedonistic world, this is a must read if we are ever to break through the self-centered society we find ourselves caught up in. This book is the best cure for depression! Terri's book takes the fear out of service. She shows us by real-life examples the many types of situations that sufferers may face and the possibilities for service they present.

In a day full of 'movement,' Terri has taught me that service starts with making room to quiet down, contemplate, and start listening to the daily promptings that, when acted upon, bring me a joy I would have missed before reading this book.

> Robbie Lawler
> National Young Mother of the Year, 1995

I meet hundreds of people each week, and so many of them, each successful and talented in his or her own way, share the same loss of direction when it comes to the basic 'how tos' of extending human kindness. It is a disheartening and embarrassing problem for many of us who want to do more. Terri beautifully shares a highly individualized, yet unifying path in *So, You're Not Mother Teresa*. In a wonderful few moments of bright, witty, and touching reading, you will have your answers as I did.

> Kim Power, founder
> Healthy Wealthy Wow

So, You're Not MOTHER TERESA

Acts of Kindness and Gifts from the Heart

So, You're Not MOTHER TERESA

Acts of Kindness and Gifts from the Heart

A guide for all women on giving gifts from the heart, featuring over 500 specific ideas.

Terri Cannavo

So, You're Not
MOTHER TERESA

© 2006 Terri Cannavo
Written by Terri Cannavo

All rights reserved. No part of this publication may be reproduced, stored in any retrieval system, or transmitted in any form or by any means, mechanical, photocopying, recording, or otherwise, without permission in writing from the publisher, except by a reviewer, who may quote brief passages in a review.

Manufactured in the United States of America.

For information, please contact:
Brown Books Publishing Group
16200 North Dallas Parkway, Suite 170
Dallas, Texas 75248
www.brownbooks.com
972-381-0009
A New Era in Publishing™

Paperback ISBN: 1-933285-50-8
LCCN 2006923329
1 2 3 4 5 6 7 8 9 10

www.auroraunlimited.org

About the book's cover image:

When combined with the book's title, this image creates a very intriguing cover that operates on many levels. The beautiful and intense blue evokes a tranquil, uplifting state which can be attained through your (the reader's) help. The ocean further represents how we (the readers) can support others and help them keep their heads above water. When combined with the title, the cover says to the reader, "Not everyone can 'walk on water' but through your help and kindness—and some wings (faith)—you can get across."

Dedication

To my loving husband, Dan and our three fabulous children, Dane, Collin, and Avery. Their consistent examples of kindness, generosity, love and joy inspire me to manifest those same qualities of living and light in my own life.

Table of Contents

Preface viii
Acknowledgements xiii
Introduction xv

Chapter 1
Joy in the Soul 1

Chapter 2
Receiving *IS* Giving 7

Chapter 3
Mary, Martha, and the Garden 13

Chapter 4
A Word about Grieving 19

Chapter 5
The Heart of Listening 27

Chapter 6
Creative Ideas of a General Kind(ness) 35

Chapter 7
Do Something! Specific Ideas for Specific Situations 51
    Abuse 54
    Accidents 56
    Addictions 58
    Being Single 65
    Chronic Illness 68

Death of a Loved One 70
Depression. 80
Divorce 83
Elderly. 89
Empty Nest 95
Funeral 98
Hospitalization, Illness and Operation 100
Homebound or Shut-in 107
Infertility 110
Long Term Care/Disability 115
Miscarriage 120
Moving Day 127
New Move, New Area. 128
New Baby—Adoption/Natural 130
Preemies. 134
Parenting (Stepparenting, Foster Care, Single Parenting). 135
Pet Loss 139
Recuperation After Surgery, Injury, or Illness 143
Suicide. 145
Unemployment (Touchy Subject) 147
Wedding/Reception. 149
Widow/Widower 151

Chapter 8
Putting the "Gentle" back in the Man 157

Chapter 9
From Local to Global 165

Chapter 10
"Mankind Is My Business!" 181

Conclusion. 187

A Note about References 191

Biography 193

Preface

I live an ordinary life filled with experiences that teach poignant lessons. I know about joy and sorrow. I know about pleasure and pain. I know about health and sickness. My story is not unique. I have surrounded myself with trusted girlfriends who nourish me when I feel empty and satisfy the girl part of the girlfriend when I'm full. There's no competition between us, just sheer contentment. I go grocery shopping, I attempt to cook, and I move the dust bunnies around. My husband is a much better housekeeper than I will ever be, but I keep trying. I exercise, I love a good read, I go to church, and I juggle the myriad of other roles a woman in today's world tries to keep in balance.

When I was eleven, I experienced the trauma of my parents' divorce. My two younger brothers were plucked out of this life prematurely at ages seventeen and twenty-six. I went to college. As a dance major, I wrenched a knee during intense rehearsals and abruptly ended my dancing career and switched to a major that went hand in glove with body movement—"Family Science." (I know. I cannot make the connection either.) My Bachelor of Science degree in "Family

Science," implies that I know a lot about whatever it was I studied in that major. At this point, I promptly put on forty pounds!

My husband and I married while I was just cutting my teeth in a career in the international shipping industry. (The dancing and family science background was great preparation for *this* career!) It was a challenging and fascinating position, offering something different every day. As an owner's agent, my department worked with a variety of ships from around the world. When the vessels would come to port, I was fortunate to be able to meet some very interesting people from other cultures. The good food we enjoyed, during the courtesy dinners we shared with the captains of the ships, didn't help the weight gain. Despite that, it was a job I loved.

In order to promote and foster my husband's career, which necessitated a move out of state, I gave up this great job and potential career. I have spent the last twenty years doing my best to raise three terrific children while supporting my husband in his career path. My actual learning of family science came from studying my own family. It has been quite a journey!

The choice to be a mom was my heart's desire. This choice comes with consequences. It means that many personal interests are put on the back burner in lieu of the interests of the immediate family. Whether one is a stay-at-home mom, a mother with a job, or a single mother consumed with her career, personal interests are often not satisfied. Some areas of personal development come to a slow, grinding halt.

I had no problem with my choice to become a wife and a mother. My decision was made from a loving and willing heart. But over the years, there was a definite emptiness that was not satisfied. When my children did not demand so much of me physically, I began to see windows of time and opportunity open. This allowed me to explore answers to such questions as "Where am I now?" and "What do I want at this juncture in my life?"

I took advantage of that time and did an immense amount of personal exploring that led me on a very rewarding, dynamic inner journey through which I discovered a deeper sense of self. That journey gave genesis to the next query of "What do I do with the growth I have experienced?" I did not recognize a new direction until I was tapped on the shoulder early last winter.

One evening a girlfriend and I were enjoying some quiet time together. We discussed all kinds of subjects, as women love to do! We were chatting about a woman we both know who recently experienced a bad fall, resulting in serious injuries. While she was recovering, she did not want people to visit her because she could not answer a phone, had a hard time getting to the front door, and she could not make up her face and wash her hair. She was more comfortable being served by her immediate family.

I readily accepted our friend's request of no visitors because, quite honestly, it was one less thing for me to do, and I simply did not know what to do for her. I asked my friend if she had done anything for her, and she told me that she and her husband had gone to visit. "What did you take with you?" I asked. "I took her some chocolates and a humorous "girl movie" was her reply. I responded, "What a great idea! How did you come up with that?" And she said, "I just thought about what I would like if I were in Rene's position. What would I like? I would love some chocolate and a fun "girl movie!" As you will read, I've found that chocolate and a great chick flick can be a wonderful pick-me-up for a variety of situations.

As I sat in silence, thinking about her reply, I was completely impressed with how creative yet simple Sherrie's suggestion was. Suddenly, I had a very strong impression come to mind that said, "You need to write a book about this." It was one of those struck-by-lightning moments that I believe comes from God. I was immediately in mental negotiations, my version of instant messaging. I responded with, "What!? Do you know to whom you are talking? I'm clueless about this kind of thing." And the answer was clear, "Terri, that is exactly the point."

I was stunned that an opportunity was developing for me to explore one of my particular weaknesses in such an exposed way. I could fall flat on my face before I even began, because I didn't know where to begin. That was my first lesson in trust. So this adventure began, very timidly at first. As I became clearer about how to present my findings and discoveries, I began to own this project mentally—and then emotionally. It evolved into a passion that has taken over much of my time. My family has been very patient!

So, as a woman, you, like me, may rediscover parts of your forgotten or even unknown self. Now what? For me, the answer was to move beyond self. I believe this to be a universal, common answer. To share what you have learned, to strengthen other people by offering acts of kindness and personal gifts from the heart. This book is written with the understanding that all women face challenges that are heartbreaking to some degree. We are trying to do our best to live a productive and satisfying life in the midst of trying situations and a stress-filled world. I hope to provide some answers that will help the trying times and painful situations become a little less trying and a little less painful.

Recently I received a phone call from a publisher, probing about the contents of this book. Her initial question was, "What makes you an expert on your subject?" I was amused by this question because I knew that the whole point of writing this book was because I was not an expert. I'm still not! I have, however, certainly improved my attitude about being service oriented. If Rene fell today and needed some comfort and support, I would make time to do some act of kindness, for I now have dozens of suggestions, listed in chapters six and seven, to point me in the right direction.

So you are not Mother Teresa. But you can emulate her example, as you spread needed goodness and cheer to those around you. Consider the following compassionate acts personal fairy dust. I invite you to come with me, as you read this book, on the fascinating journey I have been privileged to explore, to experience, and now, to share.

Acknowledgements

First of all, as I have mentioned several times throughout the book, I must give a heartfelt thanks to all the anonymous contributors for their insights, wisdom, and specific suggestions for acts of kindness. I am so grateful for their willingness to share with the readers of this book their generous and loving gifts from their hearts.

I am especially grateful for my girlfriends. They believed in me from day one when I announced that a book was in the making. My aunt Roxanne Charley, who is much more sister than aunt, has been a staunch supporter in many ways and offered encouraging words when I was frustrated and tired. Tayna Jones has always been my number one cheerleader. She has been the constant friend factor and buoyed me during our walks and soul-to-soul talks. Stephanie Boddy has believed in me and my dreams for over twenty-five years and always offers wit and wisdom that transforms our conversations into laughing fests. My daughter, Avery, thinks that I am the best mom that ever walked the earth and beams when she considers this book's reality. My mom, Judy Macy, does what a great mother does: loves and encourages unceasingly.

I must also extend my thanks to my publisher Brown Books Publishing Group. I cannot thank my editor, Kathryn Grant, owner Milli Brown, and her fabulous team enough for taking on this project and seeing its worth immediately. They have been honest, insightful, and professional throughout the process. They have calmed my racing pulse, assuaged my first-time-author fears, and allowed me to have fun while accomplishing the end result. Thank you also Ted Ruybal and Julie Zais for designing a beautiful cover and interior for my book.

In the end, I simply say "thank you" to all who have encouraged me and believed that this fantastic idea of writing and publishing a book would actually come to fruition. It was a dream I didn't even know I had.

Introduction

Many people in the world, like me, struggle with giving service and acts of kindness. It is not a question of being there for family and close friends. That comes naturally and willingly. My lack is in giving aid and assistance to the next layer of individuals beyond my familiar comfort level. When an opportunity to serve becomes apparent, my reaction is akin to a deer in the headlights. I mentally freeze up, feel a little confused, and simply don't move in the direction that would save my hide (meaning I do nothing to help, therefore I don't grow personally). I think and think and come up with nothing more than giving some kind of food, usually cookies. The cookie dough is always ready. But there are many circumstances for which a plate of cookies simply isn't appropriate. With no idea of what to do, original or not, I lose interest in the desire to help and the immediate opportunity is lost. In a day or two I feel a pang of guilt and self-recrimination, but the guilt doesn't inspire action on my part and the window of opportunity to help closes as I mentally march forward in my list of things to do for the day.

My mother thinks she has failed me. However, she is a great example of knowing how to serve others and thinking of their needs, then acting on it. For years, I have observed her quietly and lovingly contribute acts of kindness as she is able. Despite her example, since my early youth I have always felt the lack of knowing what to do in a situation where loving acts from the heart would help. I was always aware that this never came easy to me. With the immaturity and insecurity of youth, I did little or nothing to develop a desire to serve others beyond my comfort zone.

It has become obvious to me, as I have continued to mature, that my inability to be service minded must change. In a world with frequent catastrophes large and small that require more help than can be handled at a local government level, it has become necessary for all people to reach out and perpetuate acts of compassion and kindness which will help reduce stress-filled life situations. It is essential for all of us to develop an attitude of mindfulness towards action and then follow through with specific action.

The world as we know it seems to be experiencing diverse catastrophic events with increasing frequency. The tsunami in Indonesia, Katrina and other hurricanes in the Gulf States, the endless wars in the Middle East, earthquakes in the Far East, India, and Pakistan, terrorism at home and abroad, raging forest fires, drought in one season, and fearsome blizzards and storms in another season all contribute to large-scale human suffering beyond what can be imagined. The resulting cries for help from the affected communities and the people whose lives are disrupted are overwhelming. It is heartrending to see such suffering. I am confident in stating that life on this earth will continue to see these kinds of disasters. The need to answer the call to serve our fellow human beings is clear. Because of the increasing amount of disasters, I believe we must prepare ourselves for more personal involvement in the future and begin to contribute more of our compassionate energies now.

That being said, the place to learn how to do this is in the community you live in right now. I live in a community where numerous men and women regularly extend acts of kindness and gifts from the heart. They offer these acts of service as naturally as breathing. When there is a need or crisis, these individuals respond in a moment's notice with the very service that is appropriate. It is never a question of "will I or won't I"—their response is immediate. They have developed abilities and attitudes of willingness to contribute. They delegate responsibilities that are required and then quietly meld back into their lives with no fanfare or personal recognition. They are there until the situation is stabilized and the task completed, no matter how long that takes.

The service that these men and women have given and the lessons that they have learned because of their compassionate acts are invaluable stepping-stones in shaping their characters into quality people. As I have observed them in action and interviewed them, I recognized personal traits that they have in common. For the most part, these people exude a loving, gentle quality in their interactions with others. They are kindhearted and generous. You sense a nonjudgmental essence about them, which allows you to feel emotionally and physically safe in their company. A mature and loving radiance emanates from them. They are the kind of individuals that draw others to them. People naturally want to be around this kind of person.

As these men and women have served and loved, their personal involvement has heightened their awareness for detecting and attending to others' needful circumstances and unspoken calls for assistance. For example, my attention was drawn to a situation that blossomed from something small to something quite extraordinary.

Recently I read about a service project in my town, which started as a gesture of assisting a few widows and widowers with some simple house-maintenance. It mushroomed into a much larger project than initially anticipated. The project included nine homes with three of these homes undergoing extensive renovation. The volunteers donated many hours of time, labor, and money. It began as a thoughtful act of wanting to help out a couple of people but grew into a neighborhood labor of love. The neighborhood has been drawn closer together with everyone taking pride and ownership in the project.

I believe my little community is a microcosm of what is played out in thousands of communities across the world that are filled with similarly kindhearted, other- centered individuals. There are millions of good-hearted individuals who are contributing compassionate acts of service to ease the pain, distress, and suffering of their neighbors.

I have interviewed dozens of people who put acts of kindness in their daily lives. Many of them were reluctant to offer their wisdom and their ideas of service. One reason is that they felt their acts of service were obvious, boring, or too simple. They did not feel their ideas were creative or unique. I assured them any idea or suggestion was useful. I encouraged them to not denigrate any contribution they offered. What is humdrum to one person may be a spark of creative genius to another.

Another reason for their reluctance was that every one of the people I talked with did not want their names mentioned. They give their service from a pure love of wanting to help. They are not seeking recognition or credit. I have honored their request to keep their identities anonymous. I have changed some names of individuals mentioned when any examples of service are used. I am very grateful for all of the contributors' suggestions. Without their cooperation, time, and advice, the heart of this book would not have been written.

Chapters six and seven are the heart of this book. These are sections that have all the specific ideas and suggestions for service. Chapter six—Creative Ideas of a General Kind(ness)—is filled with ideas that can be used in many types of circumstances. The ideas are just that, general. Chapter seven—Do Something! Specific Ideas for Specific Situations—lists twenty-seven individual categories of needs or situations that are common among people with multiple suggestions of help and service specifically tailored to that need.

This book is written with a hope for a change of heart, a change of attitude and a change of willingness to give of your time, means, and talents. It is a place to start. The ideas are basic and the suggestions simple. My intention is not to overwhelm you on any level. This book is written especially for people who have difficulty knowing what to do and where to start, but who want very much to help. It is dedicated to those who have already figured it out.

I invite you to read these pages with an openness to learning more and a willingness to put into action the ideas that have been lovingly and generously offered.

Chapter 1

Joy in the Soul

Joy is prayer ~

Joy is strength ~

Joy is love ~

Joy is a net of love by which you can catch many souls. . . .

She gives most who gives with joy.

Joy is love, the normal result of a heart burning with love. . . .

Joy is a need and a physical power for us—even physically.

Our lamp will be burning with sacrifices made out of love if we have joy.

The best way to show our gratitude to God and the people is to accept everything with joy.

A joyful heart is the normal inevitable result of a heart burning with love.

—*Mother Teresa*[1]

---

1. Printed with permission from the Mother's Cause Office in Tijuana, Mexico.

A couple of years ago, I was driving home from a birthday massage in a contemplative state of mind. I began to ruminate on the inward journey I was actively pursuing. This journey was full of attention and activities which assisted in clearing out personal, toxic history that had been weighing me down over the years. I reflected on how much I had taken care of, how clear I was feeling, and what a lot of hard work was accomplished. It was a long and difficult road but I had made tremendous progress. All of a sudden, I blurted out "she's back!" I realized in that moment that the true essence of my soul had reemerged. I recognized the sensation immediately. It was joy!

Due to sad and unfortunate circumstances in my childhood, I had carefully and gently layered my soul's divine joy with a protective shroud. I taught myself to detach and withdraw emotionally from life on a very deep level. It was necessary for me to create that place of detachment to protect my joyful core from being destroyed. I turned away from my joyful center so I could survive emotionally. As a child, I didn't have the understanding that I could express my confusion and pain. I stayed quiet. The resulting emotional state, however, was forty years of subtle depression that blocked my ability to be fully engaged in joyfulness. The brown, murky energy laying on me was a constant state of being. It was not obvious to outsiders. It was lurking just under the emotional radar screen. It was easy to mask, easy to smile over. But it did affect the quality of my life immensely. I just wasn't aware of it because I was detached.

Until that poignant moment on the freeway, I knew I was off center but I could not identify why I was off center. Some years ago, I felt my soul getting restless. As I began to pay attention to the message this restlessness was sending me,

I knew I had some inner housecleaning to tackle. I started the journey of healing that would peel back layer by layer the shroud I had carefully woven to protect my joyful center. That freeway experience marked the moment when it was safe enough for me to allow my 8-year-old girls' joy to return in full. What a glorious moment that was for me!

I am vigilant now in maintaining that joyfulness. I know that it is a state of being to which each person is born. We are joyous, joy filled, and joy intended beings! As we grow from infancy to adulthood, we encounter life's onslaught of negative and painful experiences, which come in a myriad of ways and chip away at our natural joyfulness. A few lucky ones somehow maintain a fuller sense of joy, while others lose it entirely. The masses of humanity grope through life trying to reclaim it, not really even knowing what "it" is. "It" is joy in the soul. Joy at the core and center of the human being. It is an integral and basic substance of our souls.

As the poem that Mother Teresa penned indicates, joy is an eternal state of being that connects us with God. It is a spiritual place inside of us. To retain that joy, she writes of ways to cultivate it daily—loving, helping, giving, serving, rescuing, and living in the present moment. Each of these verbs when applied to our lives contributes to retaining that soul filled with joy, which is our natural state.

An accumulation of more and more things of the world will never satiate this longing to connect with our core and our God. Things break, rust, get old, get lost, change, and are forgotten. If you actively and consciously feed and nourish another's joy, your own joy will never rust, break, get old, get lost, or be forgotten. You will always feel whole. You may be sad, lonely, disappointed, frustrated, angry, or upset but you can still maintain your sense of joy, for that is who you are.

This book is about how to nourish your joy by serving others. Let me clarify what serving others means. I was talking to my aunt about this concept of serving others and she automatically thought of housekeepers, cooks, yard laborers, and so forth. "No, no," I exclaimed. "I'm talking about acts of kindness to those people who need a helping hand or an emotional lift." Let's be clear about the meaning of the word service. It is not servitude. It is a gift from your heart, put into action, which will lift the spirit of someone else.

Serving others is the foremost ingredient in a diet of maintaining joy in the soul. This service can be difficult, inconvenient, time consuming, and sometimes heartbreaking. But given willingly, with love and pure intent of purpose, your vessel of joy will remain full. You will be satisfied at the end of a day. You will be changed. You will be softened. You will develop a grace and radiance and light about you that will draw others to you. They may not know what it is about you that they are attracted to, but it will be the joyful core of your soul that emanates from within you.

A friend of mine said, "Most enlightened people know they need to serve." Albert Schweitzer said it this way: "Just do what you can. It's not enough merely to exist. It's not enough to say, 'I'm earning enough to live and to support my family. I do my work well. I'm a good father. I'm a good husband.' That's all very well. But you must do something more. Seek always to do some good, somewhere. Every man has to seek in his own way to make his own self more noble and to realize his own true worth. You must give some time to your fellowman. Even if it's a little thing, do something for those who have need of help, something for which you get no pay but the privilege of doing it. For remember, you don't live in a world all your own. Your brothers are here, too."[2] Serving becomes a contagious experience. The more you serve others, the more you want to serve. Today's world is hungry for individuals who serve. When people see you act in kindness towards others it gives them the courage to do the same. Pass it on, pay it forward, and perpetuate goodness. Simple gifts from the heart and acts of charity have immeasurable repercussions for spreading emotional relief and fortifying faith in the goodness of our fellow man.

---

[2] Reader's Digest Association, *Great Lives, Great Deeds* (New York: The Reader's Digest Association, 1964), 118.

Chapter 2

Receiving IS Giving

There is an old adage that states, "It is better to give than to receive." This may be true if one is promoting the morality of selflessness in a world filled with people who perpetuate the philosophy and lifestyle of "it's all about me." (Kind of reminds one of the world in which we now live!) However, for people who are yearning to manifest a lifestyle of being other oriented and wanting to raise the level of goodness in the world, the principle of equality between receiving and giving is paramount to understand.

This was a lesson learned by Miriam, who had felt very reluctant to accept anyone's help while recovering from back surgery. She had always been independent and capable of maintaining self-reliance under any of her life's circumstances and was now hesitant to be intrusive or feel needy. Miriam was taught as a child, "we'll do it ourselves." She passed that same training on as she raised her three boys. They were capable of taking care of their own! She would turn down people's offers to help, while believing she was doing the right thing. As she continued healing from her surgery, one day Miriam received a very distinct impression that she was being selfish. In this moment of enlightenment, she was taught that her selfishness denied someone else the opportunity to serve her and give of themselves. She learned she was not allowing these people to grow from their giving. She was also denying them the chance to receive the blessings that flow from compassionate service.

For the most part, we want to retain our independence and self-reliance no matter what age we are or in what circumstances we live. We have been taught to be strong individualists. Any appearance of needing help is regarded as a weakness or a lack of ability to be in control of our lives. Heaven forbid we might need something from someone.

I read an article recently by Wally Amos about this topic of giving and receiving. He concluded his thoughts with, "Giving IS receiving." It caught me off guard. I processed the thought for a moment or two and realized that he was right. The giver is rendering help and assistance. By doing so, the giver is learning the pure joy that comes from stepping outside of herself. Equally important, while the receiver is benefiting from the gifts being offered, he or she is allowing the giver to receive an opportunity for growth.

Giving and receiving are equal parts of the cycles of this life. Each of us at some time on our journey through this life will be in a position to receive service from others, as well as give service to someone else. Being in a position of receptivity is often induced by circumstances not of our choosing, therefore we feel vulnerable and powerless. This opens us up to being dependent on factors outside of our control. It's emotionally uncomfortable. When we are in the place of giving service, we feel satisfied that we are in control of our offering. We also feel we have a sense of some power and choice over our circumstances. This is the position we all want to maintain. But sometimes we don't have a choice. It's one of life's funny ways of teaching us about opposition.

However, each part, receiving and giving, is the opposite side of the same coin. They both have equal merit and value. Miriam taught me on that day of our interview, "If you don't have a receiver, you can't be a giver." It is important for us to remember the dignity and magnificence of each part.

A story told that illustrates one man's clear understanding of this principle follows. The giver in this story also taught the observers a great lesson about the dignity and joy of service.

"A committee of prominent Chicago citizens waited in one of the city's railroad stations. They were to welcome one of the greatest men in the world. He arrived and greeted them in three languages. He was a giant of a man, six feet four inches tall with bushy hair and a walrus mustache. The reception committee stood talking about how honored they were to meet him and how the important people of the city were waiting to entertain him. Reporters took down his every word. Flash cameras were busy taking his picture.

Suddenly the giant of a man asked to be excused. He walked rapidly through the crowd on to the station platform. Coming to an old woman who was struggling with heavy suitcases, he scooped up her bags with his great hands. Then he told her to follow him. He worked his way through the throng and took the woman to her coach. After wishing her a good journey, he returned to the committee . . . "Sorry to have kept you waiting, gentlemen," he said to the astonished group. "I was just having my daily fun."

The distinguished visitor was Albert Schweitzer, famous philosopher-musician-doctor-missionary. "First time I ever saw a sermon walking," said one of the reporters. A member of the reception committee remarked, "A lot of us stuffed shirts were unstuffed that moment." Well they might be. A man with a world mission, engaged in writing a profound history of civilization, was demonstrating, in a simple, unaffected way, the love of God for the least individual, and the democracy of true brotherhood."

The "very important people of the city" received two lessons that day. One, that giving service can be a satisfying and joyful experience. Two, that even "important" people can emulate this humble approach to life and have fun while doing it. From age thirty until the end of his life at age ninety, Dr. Schweitzer was devoted to serving all living creatures. It is inspirational to read about his loving attitude toward his life's work. He was unwaveringly committed to service. He displayed an uplifting and contagious attitude of joyfulness about giving of himself to others, whether high or low born.

Present-Moment Living

This story also sheds light on an important concept that Dr. Schweitzer exhibited. It is the ability to live in the present moment, being fully engaged in what is happening now. Even when surrounded by the press and important people, he was present enough to notice an elderly woman struggling with her luggage and obviously in need of assistance. He exemplified the necessity of being alive in the "now" and not allowing life's distractions to chase away an opportunity to alleviate another human being's suffering.

In recent years, "stay in the present moment" has become a very popular catch-phrase. This focused attention and attitude of being is touted with increased frequency today in many self-help books, spiritual guidebooks, and physical-training books, but it is an age-old concept. It is one of the core philosophies of the ancient yogis. Also, children throughout time and cultures display in perfect innocence a natural born ability to stay present.

When you observe children in their play or interaction with life, they are fully engaged in what is directly in front of them. Their concentration is to be admired. "Pay attention!" "Look at me!" "Are you listening?" are all phrases that we use to pull children away from this complete concentration and focus. Obviously, there are justifiable reasons for this. But to illustrate the point of staying present, consider children's ability to be completely absorbed in their present moment. If we can recapture that ability to be in the now (because we were all children once upon a time), we will reap richer and more satisfying benefits from every activity in which we are engaged. Applying the principle of present-moment living to the act of being available to serve others is essential to being truly effective.

Mother Teresa understood this principle with her philosophy of serving "one, one, and one." Serving the one is all she wanted to do because she knew that serving one individual at a time was the most effective way to help. "I never look at the masses as my responsibility. I look only at the individual. I can love only one person at a time. I can feed only one person at a time. Just one, one, one."[1] Staying present with the one you are assisting and serving gives power to the experience and changes lives.

To be truly effective in our service, we must be mentally present. It is embarrassing when you are giving of your time and talents to people, and they catch you in disinterest. It's a nice thing you offer, but when they sense your heart or mind isn't with them, they recognize you have diminished their importance in lieu of something else that has caught your attention. In their eyes, the sincerity of your love and your motivation to serve is questioned. You have compromised your integrity. Stay focused. Stay present in the moment. Let them feel they are the most important person in your life at that moment. It is vital they know that the service you give them has your full, undivided attention. Be as the small child. Stay enthusiastically engaged.

Miriam continues to be plagued with physical infirmities. Her attitude is wonderful in spite of her pain, and she is an optimistic person. She graciously allows people to give of themselves to her and her husband, Mark. He is suffering from the effects of long-term cancer. He also knows how to graciously receive service from others. He shares Miriam's philosophy on the merits of receiving and giving. Miriam and Mark, as they are able, frequently offer their acts of kindness to others. They both radiate light and love because they have a clear understanding that truly, giving is receiving and receiving is giving.

---

1. Mother Teresa. Printed with permission from the Mother's Cause Office in Tijuana, Mexico.

Chapter 3
Mary, Martha, and the Garden

The setting is in the home of Mary, Martha, and Lazarus. Christ has come to visit. Martha is concerned for the physical comfort of her guests and goes about preparing a meal. While Martha is engaged in this evidently needful activity, Mary places herself at the feet of Christ to be nourished by the spiritual food he offers.

A friend of mine, Julie, explained part of her service philosophy using this simple story. She stated there are Mary and Martha types of service that can be rendered. Martha was concerned with satisfying the physical needs of her guests. Many acts of service require physical attention; needs of food, clothing, or shelter for example. This is what Julie identifies as "Martha" service.

Mary was concerned with her personal spiritual hunger. Just as there are obvious physical needs to be satisfied, emotional and spiritual needs are also extremely important to nourish. They are not as obvious, so it becomes more difficult to observe what is needed. Many people suffer from wounds and the residual effect of scars that cannot be seen. Their cries for help are much harder to detect and are often overlooked.

Sometimes people mask their depression very well and no one would have a clue that anything was wrong emotionally. An independent soul may be drowning in an over-scheduled family life, but not know how or where to ask for help. "Mary" kind of service responds to these less obvious calls for assistance.

Each kind of service, whether it is the Mary type (spiritual/emotional comfort) or the Martha type (physical comfort), is equally valuable and useful. One does not supplant the other. They are both viable and complement the full range of an individual's needs. Mary and Martha demonstrated their perceptions of an individual's needs. Each woman offered service that complemented her individual character. We too need to have more perceptiveness to the Mary or Martha kinds of service opportunities that are all around us.

Awareness

During many of the interviews I enjoyed with my contributors, the most frequent suggestion I received, besides taking food, is to develop an awareness of others' needs. Awareness is defined as being *mindfully conscious and alert*. Many contributors said something akin to, "Observe the situation, analyze the needs, and then fill the space."

To develop the ability of being attuned to other's needs and assessing situations that require assistance is one of the first steps in mastering awareness. Pay attention to the circumstances and settings that surround you each day. Try to pick up the message or meaning of what is not being said. When you ask someone, "How are you?" be mindful of more than the verbal response. There may be a particular look in the eyes that conveys worry or upset. Body posture may be giving silent signals of "I need help." Look for rounded, defeated, sagging shoulders. Perhaps you see tension in the jaw or maybe you sense that "something is not quite right." Responses like these are red flags that indicate there is more going on inside which betrays the rote answer you will probably get of "I'm fine." Read behind the eyes and between the lines of vocal expression. I would, however, caution you not to overdo your interpretation or read too much into something. You don't want to be considered a busybody; neither do you want to communicate a message of disinterest. It's a fine line.

Many years ago Katy and her husband had moved to a new city with two small children. One day Katy went for a walk, accompanied by her two-month-old and sixteen-month-old babies she pushed in a stroller. After a while she realized she was no longer in familiar territory and had become lost. She walked and pushed, walked and pushed, thinking that surely she would find her way home any minute. Katy was hot, tired, frustrated, and worn-out from pushing the stroller. The children were miserable. They too were hot, tired, and hungry. Their crying only contributed to her personal stress and frustration. In the middle of this confusion, a couple of women with whom she had become acquainted saw her and stopped their car to say hello. Katy informed them that she was not sure how to find her way home. The women gave her directions on how to return home, said good-bye, and drove away. Considering her circumstances and obvious distress, Katy was more than a little surprised that they did not offer her and her children a ride home.

This is a simple example of not being aware of another's plight. My friend still remembers the incongruity of the situation twenty years later. To effectively comfort someone else, you must sharpen your awareness of the needs and circumstances of the people around you. It is a basic stepping-stone in developing your ability to serve others.

The Garden

After Julie explained her philosophy of Mary and Martha types of service, she expanded her thoughts to include a deeper, more intimate, long-term gift from the heart. She likened her philosophy of this kind of service to the experience Christ endured when he was in the Garden of Gethsemane. Before His torturous episode of the night's impending trial and the agonizing death on the cross the next day, He experienced personal suffering and agony in the garden that no one on earth, before or since, can comprehend. It was intense, solitary, excruciating, and long. In the garden, He supplicated his friends to "watch and pray." He sought and needed their support and attentiveness to help Him bear the heavy burden. They did try to stay awake, but each time He petitioned their help, they soon drifted to sleep again. It was a trial of affliction that was His alone to endure.

So it is with people who suffer intense trials and afflictions that can last for days, months, or even years. The adverse conditions can be long, painful, intense, and solitary. Ultimately, it is wholly personal. It is a journey on a path of self-discovery never imagined. It is heartbreaking when all you can do is be there for them, observing the struggle. Yet, sometimes that is enough. These long roads of service seemingly stretch out in front with no end in sight. It can feel disheartening and overwhelming. This is the kind of trial Julie refers to as a personal "Garden of Gethsemane."

For sufferer and server the way is long and arduous. It can be a lonely road for the server also. At times your offerings of comfort seemingly do little, from an outsider's perspective. Sometimes your intentions are misconstrued. Julie recalled being at the bedside of a dear friend, Sue, who was in her last battle with cancer. Sue and her immediate family requested Julie's assistance but felt it would not be in Sue's best interest to have other people coming and going. Sue and her family felt that she didn't have the stamina and strength to endure the constant activity. The people who did not know of the well-defined request assumed that Julie was deliberately keeping them away. They formed unkind attitudes and opinions of her. For Julie, it was a difficult time knowing others felt unkindly toward her. She persevered in her loving service because she knew her own intentions, the wishes of her dying friend, and the family's desire to protect their loved one from stressful exhaustion. Eventually the neighbors and other friends and acquaintances were made aware of the specificity of the family's desire to keep Sue guardedly cared for during her final days.

This is a poignant example of a "Garden" trial and service. Much of this kind of living is happening all around us. During these "Garden" experiences, the sufferer and the giver are being taught divine lessons that are personal and intimate. The lessons are revealed only as the traveler walks the path of experience. They are individually tailored for each person's benefit. So the giver and the receiver are mutually taught and edified. The "Garden" trial and service can provide invaluable life-changing moments.

Whether the service is an emotional act of listening, a physical act of bringing in a meal, or long-term assistance for a chronic situation, each gift from the heart honors the quiet dignity and majesty of those involved and exemplifies the better nature of humankind.

Chapter 4

A Word about Grieving

When you encounter a person who is grieving it can be a difficult, uncomfortable, or even embarrassing incident. It is easier to drop off a casserole with a minimum of contact than it is to stay with grieving individuals and allow them to display their grief. Some people find it very awkward when confronted with another's pain. They simply do not know what to do. By understanding the grieving process, we can be more effective in giving loving support to those who grieve.

Grieving isn't always associated with death. People grieve for all sorts of reasons. Grief can be due to the loss of a dream or the absence of something. For example, grief could concern a relationship one may never experience, such as not having a mate, or not knowing a father or mother. Grief can also be caused by loss of a job, a pet, or a keenly desired promotion. Grief may come from a hope for something that didn't work out, such as the above-mentioned expected promotion that the person felt was just right for him or her. Grief can be caused in ways that defy comprehension.

I recently had the privilege of getting to know Denise and Graylon, who were evacuated from New Orleans during the Katrina disaster. Their story of evading the rising waters, swimming from rooftop to rooftop in search of higher ground, contending with alligators at night, snakes in the water during the day, and surviving the chaos of the Convention Center, is harrowing! After a week of hunger, misery, and a witness of unbelievable human behavior, they found themselves on a plane to an unknown destination. They arrived in a state 180 degrees different in lifestyle from their own.

They experienced the loss of their personal history! Every physical thing they owned or with which they were identified had vanished with the flood. Their family was separated because they ended up in different states. They had nothing! They are now working on rebuilding their lives from the ground up. They are floundering through complex emotional issues, trying to find some sense and normalcy in the extreme abnormality they have experienced. Within three weeks they went from a life they knew—jobs, family, dogs, social life, and neighborhood—to a life completely different, into a place and with conditions in which everything was unfamiliar. This is loss! This is grieving at very deep levels.

When I was pregnant with our first child, my husband and I asked ourselves the question all expectant parents consider: "What if something goes wrong?" I reassured Dan that our baby would be born perfect. My husband was out of town when my water broke six weeks prior to my baby's due date. It was in the middle of the night and our families lived out of state! I just couldn't call my girlfriend with four little children to come with me, so I drove myself to the hospital. Dan made a heroic effort to get to the hospital. He arrived in time to help me through the last two hours of labor. Dane was a really beautiful baby. He had all ten toes, but there was hesitancy in the nurse's voice when it came to his hands. "What's wrong with his wrist?" I asked. "Nothing that can't be fixed," she replied. Upon close examination, Dane was seen to have no thumbs, as a result of his radial bones in his arms being underdeveloped. This new reality launched us into the world of Neonatal Intensive Care because of his premature birth and doctor visits for impending surgeries because he needed thumbs. Then just as we were emotionally geared up for dealing with the lifestyle change that comes with surgery after surgery, at eleven months old Dane was diagnosed with insulin dependent diabetes. It was a blow, to say the least!

Learning about grieving from your own experiences teaches you about the composition of grief from inside the feelings. With personal insight and acquaintance with grief, you develop an ability to express a compassion that can be healing for others as they experience their own losses. I was discussing this concept with Graylon recently. Because of his terrifying and surreal survival in the floods of Katrina, and his ability to protect himself and Denise from the horrors of the Convention Center, he knew firsthand the sense of upheaval and loss.

He and Denise are fighting loneliness, depression, boredom, and the unfamiliar. They are learning how to regain normalcy while trying to find some emotional stability and process all of the events they witnessed. In the end, they will have deeper compassion for others because of the trials they have experienced in this recent disaster. Both of my new friends know in a very personal way how it feels to be assisted and offered help under extreme and trying circumstances. With this understanding, if they choose to, they can draw from this well of experience in giving aid and succor to someone who has felt a deep loss.

Researching about grief and the grieving process educates one in the facts of the cycle from an objective point of view. Both methods of acquiring this knowledge, personal experience or personal study, are necessary because they enable one to be truly empathic while serving the individual who is hurting. Studying about grief is fine, and it has its place. However, having lived through one's own personal grief can add credibility to the love, compassion, and nurturing one can give others. This can be the virtue of experiencing the very inside of grief oneself!

In *An Etiquette for Grief,* by Crystal Gromer, she elaborates on specific ways we can conduct ourselves. In this article, Ms. Gromer states, "I've discovered there is an etiquette for grief. It is not so much a set of rules as a way of being; it requires accepting a place for sadness, for something that cannot be fixed. As a result, it runs counter to cultural assumptions that we must unlearn."

She continues, "Creating an imaginary worse scenario doesn't make the real and current one better. It trivializes it. The rest of us need to acknowledge the importance of grief and let it be, not try to make it disappear. Often we refrain from saying something meaningful because we're afraid it will hurt. Of course it hurts. But pain is not the worst thing in the world. Embarrassment isn't, either, and that should be the lesson for those who'd like to help. Evasion is worse. Forgetting is worse. The giving and receiving of solace are the most deeply human of activities. An etiquette for grief should help us live with what is hard—and share what is heartfelt."[1]

Grieving has everything to do with reconciling and coping with personal loss. It is the process of trying to reclaim some sense of emotional balance while getting on with life. The amount of time it takes to move through this process is different for every one. It could be weeks, months, or years. If the grieving individuals know that you respect their personal timetable for grief, it grants them the dignity and freedom to find their emotional equilibrium. Eventually the balance will come, stimulating a desire to engage more fully in life.

The cycle of the grieving process has been well documented by Elisabeth Kubler-Ross. For years she made it her life's work to understand the dying process, the death experience, and the grieving cycle after the loss. She identified the main stages of grief as denial, anger, bargaining, depression, and then acceptance. In her book *On Grief and Grieving*, Ms. Kubler-Ross goes into great detail regarding each stage of the grieving process.

In "Denial" we are merely trying to survive. Once beyond that stage we enter an "Anger" phase, where we begin to function again but new feelings of sadness, panic, hurt, and loneliness appear. As Kubler-Ross points out, anger can be directed at the loved one, the doctors that couldn't save your loved one, yourself for being left behind and/or not seeing the crisis coming, being helpless to stop it. We must be able to feel this anger in order for it to dissipate. As we adjust, we enter the "Bargaining" phase, allowing us a time to believe we can restore order to chaos.

---

1. Crystal Gromer, "An Etiquette for Grief," *Vogue,* March 1996, 116. Reprinted with permission from the March 1998 *Reader's Digest.*

Next, "Depression" sets in, which though heavy and dark, is usually our body's normal way of shutting down so we can adapt. Finally, we attain "Acceptance" where we learn to live with the new reality, sad as it is, and heal. These stages are not linear—they may come and go, and they may last minutes or months.

Anyone who has ever gone through a death or extreme loss knows that it feels like your heart is being ripped out of your body. It is like the whole world should stop and acknowledge your pain. I have experienced that same sense of shock and wonder. I have talked with others who have felt the same way. It is a wave of disbelief that washes over you when you realize the world continues to function on every level while you feel like you are drowning in sorrow. These are the moments of poignant grieving. They are solitary experiences. There is no help for it, but to face the grief, express the grief, move through the grief, and then somewhere along the path, let the grief rest. You are forever changed because of the grief experience.

One friend of mine who experienced the loss of her husband at any early age described her personal acquaintance with grief. "How does it feel? It is a very real physical pain. It is like nothing you have ever felt before. You can be doing anything; driving, sitting at home, watching TV, and all of a sudden this wave of grief comes over you and you dissolve in tears. One of my friends said she thought if she turned around she would see a trail of blood behind her, her pain was so great. This is normal. There is no shortcut and there is not a set amount of time allotted to accomplish it."

Perhaps with a better understanding of grief and the grieving process those of us that want to alleviate a little suffering of others can do so with more compassion. Remember, grief is a powerful, overwhelming sadness that catapults people to explore and experience other emotional offshoots that may be a surprise for them. Grief visits people for many reasons, whether it is a loss of a variety of life situations, or it is the ultimate loss caused through a death. I offer a gentle reminder that it is important to become acquainted with the grieving process because we will all grieve at some point in our lives.

Chapter 5

The Heart of Listening

Are you aware that the word listen contains the same letters as the word silent? This is a significant indicator to the kind of listening that needs to take place when you are giving yourself to others in need. It is a common human tendency that as we feign to "listen" to another's painful experience or current emotional upheaval, our minds are actually very busy doing just the opposite. We actively search for that pithy reply, sage advice (most likely, unwanted), or even ruder, a comparative story of our own. This plainly conveys to the person we are there to help that our experience was so much worse then what they are experiencing. "Just listen" was a frequent suggestion from many people I interviewed who make acts of kindness a routine part of their daily lives.

It is perfectly all right, and indeed proper, to invite the person going through difficulties and heartache to talk about whatever they feel a need to express. In your visit with them, all you have to do is create a space to listen to whatever he or she wants to say. You are not required to nor are you expected to do more than this. Often what is most soothing and satisfying to someone with a heart that hurts is to have a trusted sounding board. "Are there any feelings you would like to verbalize? Are there circumstances that you want to explore? Do you just want to talk? I am here to listen." More than anything, a soft reply of validation of some sort is the most helpful.

My girlfriend and I recently took advantage of the beautiful weather and went for a much-needed walk. We had not had the chance to just girl-talk for a couple of months, and we desperately needed to reconnect. We each took our turn expressing inner thoughts and reflections about how we perceived certain situations in our lives that seemed a little confusing. It felt so wonderful to be listened to! We both agreed it was so satisfying to bounce feelings and perceptions from one to another. We didn't need or even seek answers. Of course advice was given back and forth, but more importantly, we needed to talk and we hungered to be listened to by someone who got it. Whew! That felt great! We vowed to do this as frequently as possible.

Initially, it may be uncomfortable for you to willingly create a space for friends to grieve openly with you, to allow them to shed tears and words of anguish. Deeply felt emotions and intimate perceptions are shared during such times. Don't be afraid of the tears. Remember that crying is cleansing and promotes healing for the griever. If you listen with your heart, let your compassion show in your eyes. Hold your friend's hand or briefly touch her shoulder with tenderness. It is not required, or even desired at this time that you say anything. Just listen! Here is a list of particularly important guidelines:

- Never interrupt someone in mid-thought.
- Never finish sentences.
- Do not share war stories of someone else's similar experience.
- Do not judge.
- Do not offer advice (unless they ask for your opinion.)
- Keep such conversations in confidence.

Any of the above overtures if used lessen their confidence in your loyalty to them as a friend. They must know that they are safe in your hands. This is crucial to their healing process.

Emily Post's common sense approach to listening appropriately is good counsel. "Empty other thoughts from your mind and concentrate on what the person is saying. Then show that you're not only listening but understanding by making eye contact, nodding occasionally, and intermittently saying, "I see." If you don't understand something, ask for an explanation, a habit that comes naturally to a good listener."[1]

Remember that an effective "I see" reflects an interest in the person who is talking. Being fidgety or restless, losing eye contact, and interrupting are all dead giveaways that you simply are not that interested in the friend's thoughts or feelings. It would be better never to have offered a listening ear if you can't be truly "present" for this person. As Mary Owen has said, "Having a listening ear doesn't require supplying an answer."

---

1. Peggy Post, *Emily Post's Etiquette* (New York: HarperCollins, 2004), 281.

The heart of listening is learning to hear the quiet voices that speak to your soul in the stillness. I'm not talking about people with mental difficulties that feel they are being talked to by hostile, strange, or negative sources. I'm referring to communication of the soul to which every person has access. There are a couple of spiritual voices that I would like to highlight. They are soft and nonintrusive, but instructive.

The Intuition of Your Inner Voice

Each of us is born to this life with an inner navigational guidance tool. It is called your inner voice. This inner voice is the expression mechanism of our pure and higher self. It is a personal well of wisdom which is generated from within. If we cultivate the physical and spiritual environment of our lives, with time-tested and proven techniques, we fine-tune our receptivity to the voice of our inner selves.

At times we are afraid to follow this inner voice. As Catherine Ponder suggests, "Perhaps you have not followed your intuitive leads because they have seemed fantastic, and you have waited to reason through its promptings before you chose to act. Intuition is not concerned with reason, for intuition . . . does not explain. It simply points the way, leaving you free to take it or leave it, to heed or ignore its promptings."[2]

To help promote this distinctive listening, we must make room in our day for quiet contemplation, meditation, and prayer. When you are compiling your list of things to do, write down the time of day you will be slowing down and

---

2. Catherine Ponder, *The Dynamic Laws of Prosperity* (Marina del Ray: DeVoss & Co, 1988), 280.

turning inward. When it is on paper, as you make reference to your tasks of the day, you will be consistently reminded that this quiet time is as important as taking the kids to their extracurricular activities or the run after work. This daily practice creates the environment of stillness, where inner peace and calm flourish. In this way, we align our sensitivity to the communication frequency that is given us in soft, gentle, but very real sounds. This wisdom continuously unfolds and the more attention we give it, the more familiar we become with these whisperings. With sharpened ears we can use this wisdom to benefit other people's lives, at the same time elevating the quality of our own lives.

Promptings

Promptings are impressions you receive from a spiritual realm outside of yourself that quietly guide and cue you. They are given as prompts, instructions, or directions, which inform us of valuable information for our benefit. Often these promptings propel us to do exactly the right action for the good of another person. We just happen to be the right person for the job. These impressions can be as subtle as a feeling or a fleeting thought. For example, you may be randomly thinking of someone and in that moment receive a phone call from that exact person or information about that person that leads you to helpful action. These promptings can also be as dramatic as a clear voice in your head and as audible as talking with a friend face to face.

Do you recall in my introduction I referred to an experience of a very direct prompting? It was real, it was compelling, and it was clear. That prompting gave me the impetus to venture forth on a journey I would never have considered of my own volition. The result of listening and acting on the impression has been a deeply rewarding year of personal growth and discovery. I value every lesson I learned, most of them having to do with some aspect of giving to others from your heart. When you pay attention to the promptings and impressions you get, and then act on them, they will always benefit you for good.

I have learned to trust these promptings and impressions. I have learned to listen more attentively to my intuition. It is a distinctly subtle but powerful signal. When I pay attention and follow the guidance I am given, it always serves my best interest. The many contributors of this book have also become astute listeners to their impressions. They are familiar with how their souls hear this communication. Because of practiced trust in their promptings, many kind deeds result from paying attention to these voices of the soul.

One woman was purchasing a plant for herself and distinctly felt that she should buy two plants. Later, when she had some quiet moments, she asked for guidance through prayer regarding who needed the second plant. A name dropped into her mind. She took the plant to the woman named. The woman was surprised by the visit, but absolutely needed this act of love and attention at that time. Both women were blessed and very grateful. The first woman was blessed because she listened to her promptings and responded. Thus she was able to succor her acquaintance having no previous clue that her aid was needed. The second woman benefited from the prompting because she received a loving visit and a thoughtful gesture when she was lonely and depressed.

This is a simple example of responding to a prompting with a listening ear. It provided powerful results for the women involved. Such types of simple daily acts of kindness are generally the most frequent, because they are the most needed. Dramatic incidents usually capture the headlines. But the quiet and simple acts of love and service that produce no public attention are generated from carefully listening ears and quick responses.

Silence

We live in a very noisy world. Television, movies, cars, planes, radio, and crowds of people are all constant sources of background noise to which we have become accustomed. For example, if there is silence in the car our first reaction is to turn on the radio or put in a CD. Many people simply do not like silence. I know people who will turn on the television just to have noise in the background. They aren't even interested in what is being broadcast; they just do not want silence.

To become an effective listener, you must seek silence in your world, which promotes stillness inside of you. This stillness is the receptive center for hearing your impressions. Use stillness and quiet to your advantage. There will be lulls in a conversation. Listen to any promptings or impressions you are being given. You may receive important information in this silence with specific guidance on how to help this grieving individual in front of you. Trust these impressions implicitly. Act on them quickly if they are counseling action.

Silence is a valuable tool to use in centering yourself. Make use of this quiet time to reject anything that could be distracting your attention. Stay focused in the present moment. There is magic in the silence. There is enchantment in your inner voice and in your promptings.

Never underestimate your intuition. It is tempting to second-guess your instincts or what you sense. Be careful of being dismissive of your impressions. Learn to trust this inner, soft voice that is gently guiding your life. It has been given to each of us for personal guidance and as a source of direction to help others. Trust the impression, take action, and follow through. Once you make this a familiar pattern of living, your spiritual ears will pick up many directives that are regularly given to you. You will be amazed at how useful this resource is in guiding your daily path. Be alive to your promptings and the wonderful ramifications that will flow from that awareness. Intuition, your inner voice, promptings, silence, and stillness, create the heart of listening!

We need to find God, and he cannot be found in noise [or] in restlessness. God is the friend of silence. See how the nature—the trees, the flowers, the grass—grow[s] in perfect silence; see the stars, the moon and the sun, how they move in silence. . . . We need silence to be able to touch souls. In the silence of the heart God speaks. Let God fill us, then only we speak. Do small things with great love.

The fruit of silence is prayer.

The fruit of prayer is faith.

The fruit of faith is love.

The fruit of love is service.

—*Mother Teresa*[3]

---

3. Printed with permission from the Mother's Cause Office in Tijuana, Mexico.

Chapter 6
Creative Ideas of a General Kind(ness)

*Y*ou see the problem, you listen to your inner voice, you know who needs help. Now what? At times it's hard to know just what to do. The next two chapters are written to give you ideas you can implement. Many of the ideas that were contributed didn't fall neatly into one particular category. For general acts of kindness, the following suggestions are mentioned in this chapter to use as your own judgment and discretion dictate. A few of the suggestions, such as using notes, cards, or letters could easily be used for any of the specific categories outlined in chapter seven. Because of its universal necessity, food would also be useful under most circumstances. Some ideas may not ever feel comfortable for you to implement. I would encourage you to use your imagination to tailor any of the following ideas to express your own personality. Draw from your life experiences to enhance your personal touch. Enjoy the growth, the journey, and have a rewarding adventure!

Use a Friendly Approach

If you have the desire to lift a stranger's day and leave them feeling that they matter, you can accomplish this with a sense of play, modest humor and/or exuding a kind, loving aura. Each of us can help ease the tensions of the day. In doing so, we are serving another human being. It costs nothing. However, it does require moving your ego and self-consciousness out of the way. You will be surprised at how many people respond as if they are experiencing a refreshing breath of fresh air. Try it!

A good friend of mine loves having a bald head. He has had no hair for years. His line is "Bald is beautiful." One day he and his wife were waiting to catch a flight home and he spotted a younger Asian man sitting alone, sporting an extreme Mohawk hairstyle. He promptly walked up to the young man, sat next to him, and forthrightly asked him, "Why did you cut your hair like that?" His question was not asked in judgment, but curiosity. He proclaims that he loves being bald so much, he cannot understand why anyone would want to waste time with having hair, let alone styling it in a very attention-getting way. This question opened a conversation with the young man that lasted through their mutual flight to Salt Lake City. The young man remarked to my friend just before deplaning that the flight they shared was the most enjoyable flight he had experienced in a long time. Because of an impulsive act to cheer a stranger, my friend and this young man developed a friendship that continues to this day.

Because my friend has practiced, polished, honed, and used a friendly approach for so many years, as he gently engages strangers to feel uplifted by him he never comes across as threatening, judgmental, or abrasive. In fact, he has a look about him that invites people to participate in conversation with him. He told me it is a self-imposed, everyday assignment to seek out someone who he feels could use a little cheer. At times he does encounter suspicion and reluctance from people who simply refuse to have their spirits raised, particularly from someone they do not know. But he persists and it does not take too long before he can at least get them to smile.

I have seen his infectious delight with life and his youthful exuberance when he succeeds in drawing people out from behind their emotional walls of protection. I admire his ability to interact with people in this way. These brief interactions continue to feed his own well of personal joy, in addition to spreading joy and happiness to others as he travels throughout his day. If we have the courage, we too can learn this simple lesson of using a friendly approach with strangers as we circulate through our tightly packed days.

Listed below are wonderful ideas that will give you a place to start. As you effectively make use of any one of these suggestions you will contribute positive, loving energy into the lives of those you serve as well as continue to replenish and fill your own well of joy. This list is a beginning. There are many ideas not listed that you could add as you become aware of them. Keep the inventory of ideas and suggestions growing.

Let's talk food!

Food probably tops the list. Because food is a basic necessity, it is human nature to want to give comfort with food. Taking the time to prepare and bring food to dispirited people seems the most obvious and natural act of kindness.

This is always appreciated since stressful situations are usually times when families or individuals least want to be bothered with cooking. So we offer food. It is part of our make-up to want to take care of the physical needs of those we care about. Remember Martha? Here are a few pointers when offering food for comfort and need:

- Try to keep the food healthy. Treats are fine, but giving only sugary items is not beneficial for any kind of healing, whether it is physical or emotional. Give sugary foods sparingly, especially during a recovery period.

- Snack trays are a good idea. Finger foods are also great. These offer smaller portions for those who find eating a whole meal difficult.

- Be sensitive to the dietary requirements and needs that your intended recipient may have. For example, it is important to know ahead of time if there are dietary restrictions or guidelines that need to be followed such as those for diabetes, food allergies, medication compatibility, heart conditions, high blood pressure, and so forth. If you get specific information about a person's food restrictions, share it with those other individuals who are also contributing food items. The offerings are always meant well, but ineffective if they cannot be consumed.

- Try not to offer anything that is too rich, too gourmet, or simply too awful. Make sure that homemade food is a tested recipe that has been well received by others. If you do create something from your kitchen, use recipes you know are sure winners. If you offer purchased meals, be aware of the sugar and salt content. It may be too much for those receiving the food. Try to buy or make healthy, tasty items.

- Organize and delegate a group of volunteers who would be willing to provide nourishment for a family or an individual if the need is over an extended period of time. This helps to alleviate a cost issue, and gives more individuals the opportunity to serve. At the outset of this service, be clear about how often the food is needed so that the volunteers are ready to provide meals for as long as necessary.

- Be sensitive to cultural tastes. What is common and liked by one culture is completely unfamiliar in another. It is thus wise to have an understanding of what the family or individual enjoys and can tolerate. If there is misunderstanding, the time, effort, and money that are put into the food may be wasted.

- Deliver meals in disposable containers. There are many different plastic, microwaveable containers that are on the market today which make these offerings a "no brainer" cleanup. Also, it eliminates the need for the recipients to be burdened with remembering to return the dishes or bowls.

- Have ingredients on hand for a quick and easy recipe to whip up if you find that a meal needs to be taken in to someone.

- Use a recipe that could easily be doubled and freeze the extra portion for an emergency situation.
- Similarly, freeze any leftovers to keep on hand in case someone outside your family has this need.
- Helpful hint: make minibread, even if you don't have minibread pans. Put the dough on a cookie sheet in the shape of French bread.
- Let your children help deliver a meal or a treat to someone needing help or even just a little cheer.
- Send out for pizza and have it delivered to a family as a surprise.
- Invite some friends over for lunch, just because.
- Making a family's dinner is a nice relief for the family cook if you know that he/she has an especially busy week or is slated to give a speech, teach a class, or do something extra in his/her schedule.
- Share the produce out of your garden with those around you.
- Pick up some extra produce during the summer harvest, when produce is on sale, and share with friends, neighbors, or acquaintances. Include an uplifting note with your gift.

A Message about Notes

This was another frequently suggested idea. Notes are easy, personal, quick, creative, soothing, and can be read over and over again. My daughter has written her dad and me thoughtful, love-filled, and tender notes since the day she could pen two words together. She has given us dozens of notes over the years, for all kinds of reasons. They are some of our favorite treasures that we have collected.

Notes may be written to someone just because you are thinking about them. Leave them on the car windshield, on a pillow, on their porch, or any other creative place you know your intended recipient will find it.

When occasions arise that are of a more serious nature, notes need to be specific to the situation at hand. Notes must be filled with words of love, encouragement and appreciation. Someone having a rough time values a great quote or an uplifting thought. Remember to say something positive about the individual receiving the note. Perhaps they have a gift you admire, or they act in a way to others that is admirable. Anything specific about them will boost their self-confidence and realization that someone is thinking of them. It might be just the tonic they need to get through the rest of the day.

E-mails are considered notes, not as personal as hand written expressions, but great for extremely busy schedules. They also come in handy when you have an impulsive thought and want to connect with someone quickly. If you have to look for writing materials, the information may be gone in the time you spent looking. The spur-of-the-moment action of e-mailing saves embarrassing moments of memory lapse. It is my best communication venue when I want to act on an impromptu impulse.

Keep inexpensive cards or notes on hand. Get a year's worth of thank-you cards, birthday cards, "thinking of you" cards, etc. (See the list below.) Remember to have a supply of stamps also. Carry a few cards with you in your car, your purse, or your briefcase. Make a master list of addresses of family, friends, business associates, your church congregation, or other contacts as you feel impressed. Many of us get impressions to "act now." If we are equipped with simple materials, we can follow through on the impression and not lose an opportunity to lift someone's spirit with a note of remembrance. Send notes for the following occasions:

- Birthday
- Job Well Done
- Encouragement
- Thinking of You
- Sympathy
- Friendship
- New Move
- New Job
- Congratulations
- Anniversary
- Graduation
- New Baby
- Get Well Soon
- Retirement

General ideas for all sorts of occasions:

- First and foremost, be willing.
- Be prepared to offer help. Leave room in your day so that you have time available at a moment's notice.

Creative Ideas of a General Kind(ness)

- Give a homemade or store-bought blanket or smaller quilt that is soft and relaxing to the touch. Blankets or quilts are always comforting.
- Find out what the individual likes to read and check out books on tape from your local library that would suit this person's interest. Resupply as the need and desire continues.
- Give someone a fluffy and soft toy animal. It's like a blanket. People love to hug something close to them when they hurt.
- Offer to cut the lawn, pull weeds, plant flowers, or help with other yard work.
- Find out what a person likes and their individual interests. Put together a basket or small, clear plastic gift bag and fill it with items that would be heartwarming. (Gum, chocolate bar, a pen, a personal note, an uplifting quote, or a candle are all good ideas.)
- Make a telephone call that communicates, "I'm thinking of you."
- Present a journal to someone dealing with an affliction or other difficulty. This could be beneficial both at the time, and perhaps more so when their trial is past. Encourage the person going through a rough period to write about the experience. It is healing to express true feelings and thoughts on paper.

- Ask pointed questions. For example: "Do you need me to drive you to an appointment? Do you want company? What kind of food is appropriate to bring to you? What about your housework? May I vacuum for you? What is your most pressing need at the moment?" Any such questions that get below the surface response of "I'm fine" is what you need answered. The answers will provide the necessary information to help you more accurately assess the needs.

- Pray! Never underestimate the power of prayer! You may receive the name of someone that you had no idea needed any help or attention. Also, you may get a very specific idea of service to do for that someone.

- Show up and listen. See chapter five.

- Have baby gifts on hand. Watch the sales and have that pink and/or blue gift available to be able to grab and go.

- Keep tissue paper and gift bags on hand for the times you want to do something spontaneous for someone who might need a lift.

- Give a call to someone you think might be struggling or just needs to vent.

- Offer a potted plant with the necessary instructions for its care.

- Buy a live bush or tree and offer to plant it in their yard.

- Prepare bouquets of flowers, if you have a cut-flower garden. Take them to anyone who you feel needs a lift.
- Remember that a smile and a hello can be the easiest and most frequent act of service that you can offer.
- Join a weight-loss group with that friend who wants to lose "those last ten-twenty pounds."
- Offer service in an area of your expertise, such as counseling, law, finance, accounting, hair cutting, or music lessons. Depending on the situation, you could trade services. It helps to make people feel less dependent or in debt.
- Shovel snow for someone and maintain such caring service as necessary.
- Always look ahead at your week and know what you have on your calendar. If something develops which needs immediate attention, you will know the degree of flexibility your schedule allows. Being thus aware, you can readjust your schedule as needed. It helps avoid the "I'll get back to you" approach. In other words, plan to be spontaneous.
- Clean the headstones of the local cemetery. This service is especially effective during those times of year when attention is given to the people who have died, such as, Memorial Day and Veteran's Day.
- If you have a talent that would be helpful or useful to others, offer that service. For example, if you sew and you know someone who needs help with mending clothing or costumes, offer this help.

One friend of mine told me the following story: "I was on the costume committee for Annie Warbucks. Becky was in charge of all the costumes and she hadn't asked me to do too much. About two weeks before the play opened, I figured she must be swamped so I asked if there was anything more that I could do. She said she had it under control—she just needed to make ten more maids' aprons. I pressed her and finally got her to let me make them. I know she would have gotten them done, but I am sure she had other things to do for the play (in addition to taking care of six kids!) I like to think I was able to ease her workload a bit. Maybe she had time to do something fun with her kids that she wouldn't have otherwise."

- Solicit a teenager that you know to deliver your anonymous gifts.
- Offer to hold the shopping cart and load the groceries into the car for a mother, as she deals with her little children.
- Offer to carpool to school, sports activities, dance lessons, etc. for the family in crisis or need.
- Offer to be a chauffeur for someone who does not or cannot drive. Some situations might include doctor appointments, grocery shopping or running errands.
- Create a care package for the family members and/or siblings of those individuals who are recovering from a crisis.

- Offer to help clean and maintain some level of organization in the home during a recuperation period.
- Tie a group of colorful balloons to someone's door or mailbox to give that person a lift.
- Encourage the person going through a rough period to write about the experience. It is healing to express true feelings and thoughts on paper.
- If you are house bound or elderly but capable of limited service, consider making regular calls of encouragement to people in difficult situations who need a friendly voice. You could also make birthday greeting calls to your friends, family, former business associates, or church acquaintances.
- Consider allowing a family in need of very temporary housing during a transitional time to stay with you if circumstances are appropriate.
- Pay attention to the younger generation if you are an elderly or mature person. Compliment or nurture one that you feel could benefit from your friendship. Extend yourself.
- Share money. Give it anonymously in a card with a note of love and encouragement to a needy family or service-project fund. Have the children in your family contribute to the fund. This will encourage their natural generosity, as well as help the children feel they are important members of the service project.

- Prepare a talent show. Use your family's talents, as well as children in the neighborhood or other interested people who want to share their talent. Present it to senior centers, homebound individuals, or anyone that would enjoy this kind of cheering up.
- Organize a neighborhood party once a year. Close off the streets if it is approved, or hold it in a park. Have a couple of getting-to-know you games.
- Introduce yourself to a new neighbor and make the newcomers feel welcome. Express positive statements of the neighbors, the community, and the activities that are available. Be respectful of their desire for privacy if you sense they don't respond to the enthusiastic "welcome to the neighborhood."
- Volunteer to teach English to those who don't speak English if you have language skills. What a great service to offer to others!
- Help people from other cultures to get the resources they need, for themselves or for their families, that are offered by the community.
- Compliment someone on a talent you know they have, or when they share the talent, praise them for their efforts.
- Look for ways to bring a smile to a retail clerk who is helping you. This is easy enough to do with a sincere compliment, an easy joke, or an uplifting conversation. Treat him or her with respect.

- Volunteer to help someone who has a home business during the times of the year that are particularly busy. A woman who had a home business knitting hats was especially busy during certain times of the year as she prepared for fairs. A couple of friends volunteered to price her items and help her organize the product so that she could concentrate on finishing production.

- Offer to assist with water-heater or soft-water-systems repair if you know of elderly, widowed, chronically ill, divorced, or single individuals who may need it.

- Never forget the chocolate!

Chapter 7

Do Something!
Specific Ideas for Specific Situations

This chapter is the heart and soul of the book. It is filled with recommendations that have proven successful in easing burdens. The following ideas can be stepping-stones on your own service journey. There are twenty-seven categories which represent needs, crises, or situations that are common to the human experience.

Because a variety of people contributed the suggestions, the ideas are as diverse as the people who offered them, giving you a variety of choices. You will find suggestions that fit your time frame, checkbook, talents, and comfort level. Take the core concept of the suggestions and adapt it to your own personality. You are thus expressing your own creativity in giving to others from the heart.

In some categories, I have added statements that are especially appropriate for individuals experiencing emotionally painful situations. These statements are useful when you don't know what to say. There are also some that you simply must not say. Pay attention to these! They have the potential to hurt and to do profound emotional damage. Of course that is not your intention. Choose carefully what you say.

If in doubt, give a warm, sincere smile, or perhaps a hug, as these convey love and support.

As you use any of these suggestions, you will be learning to serve others with confidence. It is wise to have space available in your day to allow for opportunities to serve. If your days are constantly filled to the brim, and there is a real need for your service, you may feel frustrated and irritated that the service is deemed an inconvenience. Be flexible. Try to cultivate situations where you can offer your hands and your heart. Most of all, enjoy the opportunity to give from your heart.

A Word of Caution

In your enthusiasm to offer your heart and hands for another's need, be sure you do so with the intention of following through with your help. When you ask the question, "How can I help you?" be prepared for the answer. It may require something as small as washing someone's breakfast dishes and straightening the living room, or it could develop into service that will require weeks of attention.

While doing some final interviews for this section of the book, I was encouraged to meet Barbara. She had recently answered a phone call from a neighbor to assist in processing the newly arrived evacuees from Texas who had lost everything in the devastation of Hurricane Katrina. Barbara was very willing to help. This offer required her and her husband to sacrifice the time they set aside on Saturday for mowing the lawn, catching up on laundry, and doing their weekly shopping. As she moved among the shocked and numb survivors, she approached a woman named Kathy and asked, "How can I help you?" Barbara was unprepared for the answer. Kathy responded, "I can't find my children." Barbara knew in that moment that her offering was going to involve much more than assembling some box lunches and handing out clean T-shirts.

Barbara began her journey with telephone calls to Kathy's extended family in North Carolina. She spent many hours on the phone. Then there was liaison work, which included travel and local and national media coverage. She also worked with organizations such as the Red Cross, the Salvation Army, and CBS in assisting her to locate Kathy's children. After several busy days and sleepless nights, the reunion was successful—but Barbara's volunteerism didn't end there.

Because of the trust she developed with many of the evacuees, Barbara continued to assist them by finding willing, local people to aid them as they began to rebuild their lives within their new communities. Several weeks after answering a call to help and asking the simple question, "How can I help you?" Barbara was still involved in helping the evacuees make smooth transitions in a new environment.

Based on Barbara's example of selfless love and willingness to ease the way of strangers, I became aware that one must have complete honesty in heart and sincere intention to follow through to the end—no matter what is required. When you ask the question, "How can I help?" you must be prepared for whatever the answer. Finish the task initiated by the question to help. This will be a measure of your character and your true intention.

The suggestions that are listed are not designed to be all-inclusive. Obviously, there are endless possibilities, especially when you put your own personality in them. As you learn to magnify your abilities to help others, add your own ideas to the list under the category to which they apply. This will be a great reference tool to draw from for future service as you build your own inventory of experiences.

Abuse

The definition of abuse is "to treat in a harmful, injurious, or offensive way, to speak insultingly, harshly, and unjustly to or about." Abuse in all its ugly forms is unfortunately prevalent in our society today. The quiet humiliation and shame victims feel as a result of this heinous behavior is never broadcast. Many victims choose to hide the signs of abuse and excuse the perpetrators' actions. Until the victims are ready to face the truth and take action to protect themselves against these evil violations, there is not much others can do to encourage them toward healthy recovery.

In the meantime, if you are aware of abuse going on with someone with whom you have a trusting relationship, consider some of the following suggestions. One or more of them may help alleviate suffering. She may feel, with your support, that she does have a place to start to get out of the destructive pattern that has become her reality.

- Help her get professional counseling.
- Listen to her story without judgment and advice. See chapter five.
- Encourage her with the following short list of important reminders:
    o Believe in yourself!
    o You are a strong woman, even if you feel inadequately weak at the moment.

- You are not a loser, but a normal person caught in a dangerous relationship.
  - You can rescue yourself.
- Offer her a list of helpful books and/or other resources if you feel it would not be considered intrusive.
- Go with her to a support meeting. Support meetings are very helpful because the participants can perceive that, like her, other normal women are also caught in unhealthy relationships. Such meetings will strengthen her resolve to make the necessary changes and will help her to rebuild her self-esteem.
- Encourage her to extend herself to others in the group and serve them as she is able, once she has established trusting relationships. Focus on her gifts that would be beneficial to some of the other women.
- Inform yourself regarding abusive relationships. Such knowledge will provide you with a deeper understanding of the cycle of abuse and may give you insight into specific ways to help in specific abusive situations.
- Insert yourself lovingly but assertively as a friend into her life through offering your help at whatever level is needed.

One woman physically pulled her friend out of bed and forced her to help clean the house. She insisted the abused woman stay busy and get back to living her life instead of hiding. She was consistent in maintaining her friendship and offering help. Another woman offered to tend the children of her abused friend once a week for a year so that she could begin her college education. This woman eventually earned a doctorate and was thereafter able to take care of herself and raise her children.

- Encourage the abused person to extend herself by helping others. By doing so, the value of the goodness inside of her awakens and it gives her the incentive to continue to lift others. This helps to instill a confidence in her abilities and assurance of her intrinsic worth.

- Many of the ideas in chapter six can be worthwhile in offering support and love to an abuse victim.

- Bring her a delicious chocolate treat and together watch a warm, humorous girl movie! (When the timing and mood feels right.)

Accidents

Accidents are just that—unplanned and unexpected disruptions in the flow of life. They are inconvenient and extremely frustrating. Some accidents are as minor as an irritation, and others are huge events. After some, we return to the life we have known, and others actually change the landscape of our days for the rest of our lives. Whatever the case, accidents are common occurrences in all of our lives. The specifics of the situation, of course, will determine what kind of help to offer. The ideas in chapter six may also apply to many accident situations. If there is a serious accident:

- Offer to help transport family or relatives to the hospital.

- Offer to make phone calls to notify family or friends of the accident victim.

- Make sure that neighbors know about the situation (without being a busybody.) This may help to develop a support group for the family. Immediate or sporadic attention may be needed while recuperation is underway and proximity may be an important consideration.

- Check with the family to assess any help you may be able to offer regarding physical necessities from home that they will need during a possible hospital stay.

- Attend to the home if the family is going to be away for a while. Light housekeeping and any obvious yard work would be helpful. Maintaining the appearance that the home is occupied is important.

- When it is appropriate to visit, take magazines, books, books on tape, and CDs of soothing music. See the section on hospitalization for other ideas.

- Offer emotional support. Make a phone call to encourage the accident victim and/or the family. Stay in touch every few days. Even a short, "I'm thinking of you" call is meaningful.

- If the victim is a young adult, encourage other young adults to take interest in the person thus helping with the recuperative process.

- One individual suggested from her own experience to not judge the person who is injured. She had felt impatience and frustration from family and friends because her healing process wasn't as quick as they were told or as fast as they had expected. They intimated by their comments to her that there was something she wasn't doing that impeded the healing process. Remember, everyone heals at his or her own progressive rate, physically and emotionally. Don't assume this accident victim should heal at the pace you think he or she should heal.

- If the family would appreciate a helpful call to their spiritual leader for support, let them know of your desire to make this call for them.

- When the person is feeling up to interaction with you, take them a yummy chocolate treat and a warm, humorous movie!

Addictions

"It takes a big heart to help an addict."
—*Julie*

Both the addict and those who love them suffer. Because the world we live in is infused with people who have addictions of all kinds, there is much suffering that occurs and millions of people are affected by addiction behaviors and consequences. Some time in our life there is a high probability one of the following situations will develop: we will become aware of one or more people we know who are addicts, we will be affected personally by an addict's behavior whether we know them or not, or we will have complicated relationships with an addict.

Whichever the case, it is reasonable to encourage people today to increase understanding of addiction and codependency. With familiarity, knowledge, and more awareness of the destructive nature of these serious and negative lifestyles, we can be more affective in minimizing the disruption these behaviors have in our lives and the lives of those we love and want to help.

There are many useful and informative resources on the Internet that address this topic of addiction. I use the following information from a site called Visions. Addiction is a dependence on a behavior or substance that a person is powerless to stop. Addiction has been extended to include mood-altering behaviors or activities. Some researchers speak of two types of addictions: substance addictions (for example, alcoholism, drug abuse, and smoking;) and process addictions (for example, gambling, spending, shopping, eating, and sexual activity.) There is a growing recognition that many addicts are addicted to more than one substance or process.[1] The following quote gives more insight on addiction and the common occurrence of a behavioral interaction family and friends develop with the addict called codependency.

> Codependency is a term often used for the spouses, children or other family members of the addict. When people become codependent, they begin to focus their lives solely around the addict. They make

---

1. http://www.visions.ab

decisions based on if the addict will affect any possible situation positively or negatively. They begin changing their own behaviors based on the addict's behaviors or wishes. Families, friends and employers of addicted people often don't understand an addict's seemingly chaotic mindset. They witness the addict behaving in perfectly normal ways, arriving at work on time, paying bills, and spending time with their family and then the next day or even the next hour the addict becomes immersed in the depth of their addiction again. When addicted people feel the need to feed their addiction, they think of nothing else. Their one thought, their one urge is to indulge their craving. It is during these times that the addict is in their most irrational and uncaring mind set. When the urge to indulge their addiction has taken control, they are concerned only with satisfying that enslavement, absolutely nothing else matters. They will miss work, abandon their family, and neglect their own health in their pursuit of a fix. The future simply does not matter and they do not consider the negative consequences that will come about as a result of their single-minded focus.

The following suggestions are directed toward aiding and sustaining the addict's support system (i.e. family, friends) and the addict through their difficult times:

- Encourage the individual in their recovery process. Offer emotional support. Let them know they have what it takes to stay whatever course they chose.

- Do not judge nor criticize those who love the addict. These people need positive feedback. Love them and reassure them that they are wonderful people.
- Send a card with the message, "I'm thinking of you."
- Stay in touch with positive, uplifting conversations in frequent phone calls.
- Lend a listening ear. See chapter five.
- Don't try to fix it for them. Sometimes a spouse of the addict hasn't figured a way out of the relationship, or if they choose to stay, hasn't figured out how to live with their reality. They need to have someone to talk to about their situation. Many times, these support people glimpse the true and wonderful nature of the addict. They cling to the fantasy and expectation that "one day" the addict will live life from that part of himself or herself on a regular basis. That hope is what keeps the support people involved with the addict, even though they know intellectually that it is a harmful relationship.
- Refrain from asking questions such as, "Why don't you tell them 'this' or 'that'?" or "Why do you put up with his or her behavior?"
- When visiting with parents of a person dealing with drug addiction, mention the good qualities and characteristics of their son or daughter. The parents need to know that the addiction is not all that people see in their child.

- Offer any healthy act of love and service that you think would be appropriate. It sends the message of "I'm thinking of you." This is sometimes all that is needed to give them the courage to face another day. See chapter six.

- As you are able, encourage the support system of family or friends to learn how to serve the addict effectively.

- One woman who was in this situation suggested it is very important to know how to balance your life. Coping with an addict is very consuming, both in time and in the emotional arena. If you don't pay attention to your own needs, you can easily become resentful and empty of feelings of love or wanting to help. You have no energy to give anything to anyone, and you lose the ability or desire to grow personally.

- Help your friend to focus on balancing her life by encouraging her to engage in activities that she enjoys doing. Give her opportunities to do what she wants or needs to do.

- Pay for and book a manicure or pedicure for her.

- Offer to pay for and book a massage! (Make sure she doesn't mind being touched by a stranger.)

- Reassure this person that he or she is not crazy! A very important suggestion I received from several women.

- Invite this person to healthy social gatherings that you know she would like.

- Encourage family and friends to learn about their addiction.
- Establish and maintain firm boundaries with the addict. Do not equivocate. Do not vacillate. The "tough love" method is important to maintain with this approach.
- Do not rescue the addict! It is very tempting to want to help by relaxing the boundaries when you see them having extremely difficult times during the recovery process. It is uncomfortable to observe as they attempt to remain strong, go through withdrawals, or struggle with extreme emotions. Be careful to understand it is you that is being assuaged if you rescue them. You are doing the addict great harm if you rescue them. The progress they are making has then been compromised. You are now pegged as someone they can take advantage of when they want to manipulate a stressful recovery situation to their benefit. They now have the upper hand. Codependency rears its' head in these situations.
- Attend twelve-step programs with the addict. It will give you a real insider's point of view and also educate you in specific ways that will help you encourage the addict to stay strong and focused on his or her recovery. The twelve steps are:
  o Admit powerlessness over the addiction.
  o Believe that a power greater than oneself could restore sanity.

- - Make a decision to turn your will and your life over to the care of God, as you understand him.
  - Make a searching and fearless moral inventory of self.
  - Admit to God, oneself, and another human being the exact nature of your wrongs.
  - Let God remove all these defects from your character.
  - Humbly ask God to remove shortcomings.
  - Make a list of all the people harmed by your wrongs and become willing to make amends with all of them.
  - Make direct amends with such people, if possible.
  - Continue to take personal inventory and promptly admit any future wrongdoings.
  - Seek God through meditation and prayer.
  - Carry the message of spiritual awakening to others and practice these principles in all your affairs.[2]
- Help the person locate and use the community resources that are available (i.e. counseling, lawyers, support groups, etc.)
- Do not judge the person.
- One woman noticed while she was in the hospital that the medical staff was very generous in doling

---

2 http://www.12step.org

out pain medication. It was very helpful when she needed it, but after a while she felt mentally fuzzy and physically not in control. She reduced the amount taken and felt more pain, but less dependent. She cautions overuse of prescription drugs.

- Enjoy a delicious chocolate treat together and a warm, humorous movie!

Being Single

I had not even considered this category until one of my girlfriends pointed out to me that many single people get swept to the sidelines of life. They may have willingly chosen to remain single or have not had the opportunity to choose a partner. Either way, being single is a tough status for some people and they can get lost in our family- dominated society if we are not careful to include them.

Obviously, there are always those individuals who love this lifestyle choice and thrive within it. They can usually assuage their loneliness and aloneness with confidence and capability. They have figured out what fills them up or satisfies their emptiness. However, every now and then they need a loving nudge from someone, sometime, to get them out of their "singleness" thinking and enlarge their scope by helping others and letting others help them.

My girlfriend has a loving and wonderful sister who has never married. They both received great learning experiences when her sister lived with her and her family for several years. Shay enjoyed the caring, loving attention and help Kappie gave her children. The children observed another terrific female role model as they developed an intimate life-long love and friendship for their aunt, and Kappie learned about the dynamics of these relationships while being part of a young family. Although this living arrangement was extremely difficult and stressful for everyone, it was ultimately a complete win-win situation. There were many occasions when personal interests were sacrificed for the good of the whole family unit. Everyone learned meaningful, and sometimes painful, lessons of the importance of living a more selfless life.

Of course, not all single people will have a similar positive experience, nor would some want to even entertain this kind of arrangement. But it is an option. Here are some suggestions to consider when you have an opportunity to serve a person who is single:

- Probably the easiest and most effective thing to do is give them a phone call with a message of "I'm thinking of you" and expressing genuine interest in their day-to-day activities.
- If distance is an issue, drop a note in the mail every now and again. Give suggestions for a great read, a new recipe to try, or a movie you enjoyed and would recommend.
- Invite them to family gatherings as much as is comfortable. Seasonal celebrations are very important to maintain traditions and memories for some people.
- Set up a tradition in your life with this person to have them to dinner on a weekly or monthly basis.
- Invite a single person you know well to prepare a dinner for your family every now and then.

- Suggest a "country of the month" idea. Have everyone in the family contribute to the meal.
- Let the person demonstrate or even teach you or your family about a special skill or an interest at which they excel.
- If this single individual is musically inclined, invite them to share their musical talent with your family and/or friends on occasion, such as holding "musical evenings."
- If there is a certain level of trust and a known history of the single person, let that special person contribute to the lives of your children in an inclusive way, such as reading with the children, tending the children when you go on a date with your spouse, helping with school assignments, and being invited to share in some of your family and holiday activities.
- Invite/include this person in your community, faith, or civic activities as well as book clubs, hobby classes, and other such group happenings.
- If there is interest shown, introduce this person to your circle of friends.
- Suggest they participate with you in charitable work in the community.
- See chapter six for ideas that would be appropriate for someone in this category.
- And of course, enjoy an evening together with a chocolate treat and a warm, humorous girl movie.

Chronic Illness

This is a difficult category, simply because "chronic" means long-lasting, persistent, and recurring. Cancer, neuropathy, bipolar conditions, AIDS, burns, heart problems, MS, Parkinsons, and obesity are just a few of a long list of chronic illnesses that plague people. The support systems for these people can become strained over a long period, and the loved ones just get worn out. It is very needful to offer appropriate assistance during long months and sometimes years of maintenance and/or recovery for the victims/patients and their families.

A friend of mine has cancer. He has a remarkably positive spirit and exudes an upbeat optimism. He and his wife have undertaken a very daunting and serious battle to overcome this disease. One of their friends was simply unable to verbalize to him face-to-face her feelings of sadness that he had to deal with this harsh reality. She wanted very much to let him know of her support and love. Thus, one day my friends found a package on their doorstep filled with "Mr. Incredible" trinkets and gadgets that conveyed to them her deep feelings of sorrow for their trial. At times, we need to find ways to serve with which we are comfortable. Here are some more suggestions:

- Sometimes with long-term care, the recipient needs to establish a trusting relationship with the person who offers his or her service over a period of time. This could be seen as a testing period. The receiver may suggest small needs at first to determine if, in fact, the one serving will follow through. It is disappointing to depend on a person for a needful act, only to realize it is not going to be considered needful or followed through by that person.

- Treat the person with respect and dignity. Don't act as if the person is dying or at death's door. This is one reason some people may not want to volunteer information about their health situation. They want to be treated as they have always been.

- Send notes or cards on a regular basis with uplifting, inspirational, and positive thoughts.

- Offer to sit with the person, if needed, during difficult times of the day or night. This also helps relieve the long-term caregiver.

- Regularly run errands for the person and/or the family if they are unable to get out of the house. For example, pick up groceries, go to the pharmacy, take them to doctor appointments, or purchase small household items.

- Repair and maintain the home as needed. If the job is too big for you, enlist the necessary help—after receiving permission from your patient that it is okay.

- Stay in touch on a regular basis with cheery and uplifting phone calls. Refrain from asking, "So how are you today?" with every conversation.

- Offer to take care of their pet or pets on a regular basis if your time and distance allows.

Chronic illness can also be a major financial strain. A great service, apart from giving money, can be organizing fundraising events. Following are some ideas:

- When children in a young cancer patient's neighborhood would hold birthday parties, they would ask for donations to his cancer fund instead of accepting presents for themselves.
- Sponsor a lemonade stand for children and give the raised funds to the ailing person.
- Have a bake sale and donate the funds to the family of the chronically ill person.
- Sell bandanas. Consider imprinting a personalized message on the bandana that inspires people.
- Currently, rubber bracelets with personalized messages are popular. These could be sold with the person's name engraved. Donate the funds to the family or person.
- Enter a sponsored marathon or walkathon.
- This is time and case sensitive—take a chocolate treat of their choice, and include a warm, humorous movie!

Death of a Loved One

There is nothing in life that prepares a person for the departure of a loved one. It is unnatural to our sense of continuity and the familiar. Even when the loss follows months of declining health and you know intellectually that that person is going to die, when the moment of death occurs, it almost seems a surreal experience. Perhaps nothing is more heartbreaking then losing a member of one's family or someone else extremely close. Shock sets in immediately, and it is difficult for the mind to grasp the reality of what is evident—that your loved one is not coming home. When death becomes a part of your life experience, deep lessons can be learned. There is the lesson of coping with loss, the lesson of discovering the depth of your own emotional strength, the lesson regarding your own mortality, and the lesson of compassion.

If you have not yet experienced this particular personal loss, the listed suggestions will help you feel a little more comfortable when your desire is to comfort the mourner. The family is usually exhausted and emotionally spent, so keep visiting brief. Refrain from lecturing, trying to comfort with stories that "are worse then this," or staying too long. Acknowledge the person's and/or family's pain and let them talk, cry, or vent their anger. A hug, simple words of comfort, and expressions of love and support are appropriate. It all helps.

It is important to remember to visit the family when you are feeling strong, especially if you too have been emotionally affected by the passing of their loved one. It is unfair to go and offer your condolences, and then when you are overcome with emotion, receive consolation from the family! It is worthy to mourn with those that mourn, however you do not want to end up burdening the family with your grief. That is not the reason for your visit.

Everyone has a personal way of handling grief. Some people want to keep busy and avoid home where memories are most tender. Some individuals want only to stay home and for a period of time avoid interaction with others. Others may not want to be left alone at all.

Two women in the same neighborhood lost their young husbands within months of each other. They both have families that include several little children. One woman did not want to be without her kids. She found strength in their companionship and their energy. She needed them around her. The other woman found it soothed her emotional state to have some time away from the children. She needed the quiet to help center herself and the physical rest allowed her mind to settle and her body to regain strength. In whatever situation you encounter, remember to be sensitive to the needs of that individual or family. One person's needs may be exactly the opposite of someone else's needs, as in the above example. Ask specific, but sensible questions, which will help you get clear answers. For example, "May I take your children overnight?" If the answer is that she would rather keep her children close, offer to lighten some physical burden. Keep an eye on those who are grieving and respond according to their needs.

Don't be afraid to call. Don't hide. This applies even if you do not know the individual or family who has just lost a loved one. Sometimes friends or acquaintances disappear following a tragedy because the impression is that they believe their friend or friends need time to grieve. They don't need to be abandoned! Observe respectfully from a slight distance, but always with the intention of being there for them at a moment's notice.

My cousin, Karen, was relating an experience she had of assisting an elderly woman in the last days before she died. Initially, with some reservation and questions, she agreed to help this woman. For several months she gave physical, emotional, and spiritual comfort as the woman continued

Do Something! Specific Ideas for Specific Situations

to decline. My cousin was at her bedside with the woman's family when she died. Karen gets emotional relaying this story because, as she served, she learned to love this woman unconditionally. She also realized what an honor it was for her to share in this very sacred experience called "death." She says, "Everyone wants to be present at the beginning of someone's life—why not the end?" My point here is to encourage us not to be afraid of the anticipated death. Offer love, a generous heart, and gentle service to the one who is transitioning from this life. The lessons will continue to flow. It is a gift that the dying person leaves with you. Even if your efforts feel inadequate, do something!

- Call and check regarding the convenience of stopping by to give comfort to the family.
- Offer to make phone calls, if appropriate, to inform friends or distant relatives or out-of-town family.
- Stop by to give a hug. Perhaps simple condolences are appropriate for the moment. When the moment is right, just listen to their grief or comments. See chapter five.
- One woman showed up with a mop and cleaning supplies. She invited the widow to go to her bedroom for a quiet rest, to read or relax, while she cleaned her house.
- Taking this idea one step further, organize help to have the house cleaned, dinner delivered, and the children occupied with friends. This service would allow the parent to have needed time to him or herself.
- A recently widowed acquaintance suggested the above idea was wonderful, however, for her it was

important to also have an activity preplanned. She felt that having alone time was too painful and she needed an activity that would distract her. She appreciated the efforts of her friends when they would create space for her to be by herself, and would also give suggestions or plan something for her to do during that time away from the demands of home and family.

- Often the family doesn't want to leave their home. The traffic, noise, and crowds can feel overwhelming. Offer to run some errands for them.

- Be sensitive to visiting too long. These longer visits should probably wait until after the funeral.

- Get help or do some of the yard maintenance. A clean and neat yard is easy on the eyes when the family comes home from errands. This isn't something people are inclined to take care of when death is lingering.

- After time has passed, don't forget your suffering friends. Give them a call, especially on the anniversary of the death of their loved one.

- Keep a calendar of events that have transpired so that you can remember to stay in touch at the appropriate and meaningful time of year.

- When time has elapsed after the death, food offerings may continue to pour in. Remember to keep the food healthy and nutritious. No one needs extra sugar or sweets available all the time. One woman said she felt the thoughtfulness was generous, but she and her children didn't need the extra calories. She found it difficult to turn down generosity, because she didn't want to hurt feelings. She preferred healthier food if it was going to be given to her family.

- Along that same line, if the main provider of the home died, consider giving the family money instead of providing meals. The meals are thoughtful, but the family, knowing their own intimate needs, can use the money in specific ways that alleviate some financial strain. (This is a great suggestion after the shock has lessened, and life begins to resume to a somewhat normal pace.)

- Instead of bringing in meals, buy gift certificates for local restaurants, grocery stores, or other local stores you feel would help the family or individual.

- Poetry is helpful and sensitive. Give a book of poetry and present it in a beautiful wrapping.

- Send letters, cards, or notes with uplifting themes. Keep the message positive.

- Get baby sitters for the children and keep them occupied. Sometimes they get neglected or are in the way. This can help distract their attention from the tragedy.

- Bring healthy breakfast food. This is seldom remembered.

- Bring light snacks and grazing foods. These are good items to have on hand, as sometimes a big or heavy meal is not what the family has the appetite to eat.

- If applicable, help the person find something on which to focus his or her mind to keep it active and functioning. This is helpful as often the mind is unable to stay focused for very long.
- At the grave site, put anonymous flowers whenever you think about it.
- Allow mourners to confide anything, and remember to keep your tongue quiet.
- Wait a week or two and then check back with the family. Take a meal in when others are no longer offering help.
- Flowers are always welcome. Make sure there are no allergy-sensitive people.
- Green plants in pots will be a lasting memory after the blooms fade from bouquets. Make sure there are instructions as to how and when to water and how to tend to the plant.
- Keep sympathy cards on hand. They aren't the cards that we normally would have handy, but are very good to have ready to send as soon as you hear of the loss of a loved one.
- On the day of the viewing, offer to take in a meal before or after. The family is always exhausted and may not take the time to eat. Note: bring food that is nourishing. A platter of cut up fruit and vegetables is great. Several kinds of small finger-sandwiches are wonderful. Refrain from heavy foods or too much sugar. The family's stomachs are already churning and this kind of food is a poor choice at this time.

- After the passing of a loved one, help clean and organize the home. If it is an elderly relative, select special treasures and share the stories. Help pack and then clear away boxes and leave the area tidy.

- If death and the funeral occur out of town, cleaning the home of the one who is experiencing the loss can be very helpful. Sad and unexpected news such as this creates the need to drop everything and depart for the destination. It is so appreciated to come back to a house that is clean and organized.

- Write a letter to the grieving family about the loved one's influence in your life. Give specific examples.

- If you have scrapbooking or video skills, put together a photo album or video with pictures, meaningful songs, etc., along with letters and stories as a memory for the family and a tribute to the one who has died.

- Make a CD of music that is soothing and meaningful to help the grieving process.

- Keep phone calls infrequent and short.

- Refrain from asking personal or detailed questions regarding the circumstances surrounding the death. If the family member wants to share these intimacies, they will do so on their own volition.

- If the death occurs in the home and smaller children are involved, suggest that you take these children to your home for a while as the family gets details planned.

- Purchase a bleeding heart bush and plant it in the yard of the family with their permission. Include a note or letter that reflects your positive feelings about the deceased.
- Make a pillow out of some of the deceased's favorite clothing.
- Have a pleasant and appropriately positive attitude. Grieving is exhausting. Try not to be exuberantly cheerful.
- After the funeral, stay in touch with the family. Do not overdo your attention, however. Drop in a meal once a week. Make a quick phone call. Offer to go for a walk with one of the family members. Talk about other things than just the situation. Most people don't want to feel like the "local charity case." One gentleman got sick of people always asking, "How are you doing?" even months after his wife died. He just wanted to be treated normally again. Be sensitive about knowing when to stop inquiring after their emotional state.
- Offer to help fold clothes and clean out personal effects of the person who died. This is difficult for family members to do as the wound is raw, and they recollect their loved one in the clothes and using the personal items. If the clothing is not to be distributed among the family, perhaps take them to a shelter for people who could use the items.

- During Thanksgiving dinner, one family member began the meal with remembrance of the departed loved ones and mentioned his gratitude and love for all those at the table because of life's uncertainty not guaranteeing that all of those present would be at next years' dinner.
- Verbalize your positive memories of the departed to the family.
- Share experiences with the family or individual of how you have handled the death of a loved one. Do this after the funeral when there is not so much for them to think about. Be sensitive to its usefulness.
- When appropriate, and if you know them well, include them in service that you are doing for someone else.
- If you are a close and trusted friend, sort through the mail. Eliminate the junk mail and simplify and organize the remainder into orderly piles of bills, correspondence, magazines, and so forth.
- Bring them a terrific chocolate treat and share a warm and humorous movie after an appropriate amount of time has passed.

Speaking to someone who has suffered a great loss, especially if you haven't experienced a personal loss yourself, can be uncomfortable and awkward. In most cases, be sincere and go with what your heart tells you. Still, some things are better left unsaid. The following are things not to say:

- "Well, at least . . ." These statements are meant to console, but they leave the brokenhearted individuals with a feeling of hollow condolences.
- "He or she is better off now. He or she suffered so much."
- "Now you can get on with your life."
- "Boy, you sure have a lot of lonely years ahead of you."

These comments may leave the mourner depressed or offended. On the other hand, several phrases or comments can uplift, inspire, and soothe. Try some of these appropriate things to say:

- "I'm sorry for your loss."
- "May I bring you dinner tomorrow night?"
- "She was such a wonderful person."
- "He was a great example to us all."
- "I would love to help with your services. May I greet your guests, or make phone calls for you?" and so on.

Depression

Depression is a difficult life situation. Sometimes depression occurs because of a chemical imbalance that may be corrected with the right kind of medical attention. Other times, depression can be as temporary as a few hours or days. Sometimes it can last for months based on issues that may be outside a person's control, such as loss of a job, loss of a loved one, illness, etc. It is not necessary to know what caused or contributed to the depression, but it can be helpful to those who want to render assistance. It may provide an idea of what kind of service would be most helpful.

One woman said she kept returning to the home of a friend she knew was at home and was experiencing a deep depression. She would knock and knock again with no answer, then leave a simple gift at the door. She told me it took about seven attempts before the friend had the courage and energy to open the door and invite her to come in. Her friend apologized for being so evasive, and she expressed her appreciation for her friend's persistence in coming again and again to leave a gift of love and thoughtfulness. Eventually the depressed woman was persuaded to get involved in some charity work herself and share her gift of needlework. This service was a beginning step in counteracting the depression she felt. It helped pull her out of the darkness she was experiencing.

Sometimes it does take persistence to make a difference in a depressed person's life. But by offering ongoing, loving, nonjudgmental gestures from the heart, such persistence may bring a measure of needed relief. The friend's depression may not be completely lifted, but your consistency does let the person know you care. It may engender strength and determination to do something to move out of the darkness. Your efforts do matter. Here are some ideas:

- Explain the situation to the children at their level of understanding (regarding the parent suffering from depression, assuming you have a relationship with the family and have their approval.)
- Involve the children with your children in healthy and meaningful activities such as outside sports

activities, simple community service, or music lessons if appropriate.

- Keep the children busy. Give them responsibilities around the house to alleviate the parent's load.
- Offer to drive the depressed person to doctor appointments.
- Send the person notes with positive quotes, funny sayings or encouraging words. Make this a weekly occurrence as long as you feel it is appropriate and is something to look forward to as the tradition develops.
- Take your friend to see someone who is also in need of a visit—perhaps a homebound individual or someone who is recovering from surgery. The list of reasons is endless. Loving service usually lifts the person who lifts another!
- Be persistent. The depressed person may not want any visits. You may get rejections to your offers of help, using a myriad of reasons. Keep going back. Reassure the person of your love. Be gentle in your voice and sincere in your offerings. Eventually you will gain the trust the person needs to know you are honest in your desire to help.
- Try to discover a talent or gift this person has that could be useful to others. They may be willing to share it with others who are in need.
- Offer or arrange for occasionally needed assistance with housekeeping for a person in which a chemical imbalance causes sporadic mood changes.

- Encourage those on prescription drugs to be consistent with their medication.
- Tape a church or spiritual meeting for the "shut-in" and present the tape that same day. Such a thoughtful act will surely be uplifting.
- One woman had witnessed her friend go through a particularly difficult year with surgeries and recovery. She purchased a sailboat and gave it to her friend on her birthday with the note, "This is a symbol to remind you that 200_ will be a smooth sailing year."
- Many ideas listed in chapter six are very applicable in this category.
- Share a delicious chocolate treat and a warm and humorous movie with this friend. The light and fun energy of the movie will help relieve some heaviness of spirit, and of course, chocolate is always soothing!

Divorce

Who among us has not been affected by divorce? It surrounds us. Someone we know has experienced it. Perhaps even you, the reader, have walked down this pain-filled path. I had a discussion with a girlfriend who was in the middle of a divorce. I wanted to draw from her an insider's view of the process and the main emotion that she experienced most frequently. I readied myself for "deep despair," "unbelievable anguish," or a similar reply. I wanted to make sure I had an appropriate empathic response. She said, "Relief!" Uh, what?

We had a good laugh over the disparity of the answer I had anticipated and her opposite response! However, it did cause me to reflect on the fact that there are innumerable situations which result in divorce.

In my friend's case, she was the one to initiate the separation. She was not dealing with the emotional impact of being served divorce papers. However, this doesn't mean that such a one isn't reeling from the loss of the relationship and mourning the death of a marriage. Because each divorce has its own set of circumstances, the emotional gamut could vary from immense relief to abject guilt and sorrow. As my friend was in a state of relief and didn't need to be bolstered with empathic listening, she still valued support from loving and caring friendships. It is thus important to be aware of the person's current emotional state. With this understanding, you will be better able to render appropriate support.

A second situation may be one in which both parties agree to the dissolution of their marriage. Even though both parties are in accord, it is nonetheless common to feel loss, perhaps also some guilt, and a sense of failure. There may be issues that are not agreed upon, resulting in anger and/or frustration. With this major life change, the process of separation and the road to healing afterwards is always difficult. It carries a wide range of negative emotions, from being emotionally upset at the least, to feeling awkward, experiencing unclear thinking, or encountering uncomfortable confrontations. Offering a stable friendship, support, and encouragement is always appreciated. The third possibility is the person did not want the divorce. In this situation deep pain, guilt, anger, and resentment would likely dominate emotions during the process of separation. These individuals would most likely be fragile as they try to cope with a sense of self-worth. It is difficult during this time to feel valued and loved because of the glaring rejection that divorce implies. A great support system of encouragement and love is highly recommended with consistent follow up and maintenance of friendship and attention.

The sense of loss and failure for each of the above possibilities is an overriding emotional factor. The poignancy of that loss may in fact be just as acute for those who want to separate as for those who do not. The key for the service-giving individual is to remain neutral to both parties and exercise the wisdom of being nonjudgmental. Supportive love and a caring attitude will soothe many levels of pain.

There are many resources available with valuable information that sheds light on all the different dynamics of divorce. If you feel you would like some enlightenment on any aspect of this life situation, it would be wise to do your homework. A clearer understanding will give you a measure of validation as you try to comfort. You cannot know exactly what the individual is feeling, but a basic and fundamental familiarity with the relevant aspects of divorce is extremely beneficial to your effectiveness.

The following suggestions are offered as a neutral place to stay in these uncomfortable times. The proposed ideas are appropriate for both males and females moving through this difficult time.

- Establish a connection with these people immediately. Love them and reassure them. Be aware of their sense of embarrassment and their feeling of a loss of self-worth.

- Stay out of it!
- Do not change the way you treat them. Continue to be caring and polite. Wave, chat, make eye contact, or drop a note of encouragement in the mail.
- Do not judge either party!
- Volunteer to watch their children, when appropriate, such as when the parent has a meeting in the home that brings up divorce details. In such a situation, it is advisable to have the children out of listening range. Such meetings could include private meetings with counselors, lawyers, or clergy.
- Be proactive in helping the parent find a good, trusted baby sitter if the parents do not have one. In such an effort, try to find one that comes highly recommended with appropriate skills and experience. There may be times the parent just needs a change of scenery to help reduce the anxiety and stress.
- Be ready to listen to their story. Refer to chapter five.
- Offer to take this person to lunch, a movie, or a quiet place for a visit. Just get them out of their routine for a break!
- Ask the individual, if he or she is the primary caretaker of the children involved, what are their needs regarding household functions. Such needs may include limited childcare, house cleaning, meals brought in. Offer what you can if it is appropriate.

- Encourage your friend or friends not to make rash decisions that will affect them long-term, such as immediately selling the house, changing the children's schools, quitting work.
- Suggest they find a positive support group if you feel it is appropriate. Consider going to the first several meetings with them to ease the way into a strange environment. Although it may be initially intimidating, the benefits of a support group are great.

"Eventually, even the best friend will burn out, though: long before you're ready to stop talking about your divorce, your friends will have tired of hearing about it.

The benefits of joining a support group—or going for individual therapy if you're not ready for the group experience—cannot be overstated. A good support group is not "a bunch of whiners" or a forum for male or female bashing. Rather, this is a collection of people at various stages of the divorce-recovery process who can offer advice, assistance, and the reassurance that your negative thoughts and feelings are completely normal—and that they will pass. Members of a divorce-support group have stood in your shoes, and can demonstrate by example that a better future is just around the corner for those willing to take the steps to get there."[3]

---

3. http://www.divorcemagazine.com

- Encourage them to rekindle interest in previous passions they had, such as ceramics, dance lessons, hang gliding, hiking, martial arts, painting, or papermaking. The list is obviously person-specific. Try to draw from them their interests and help them get started again.
- Offer to put the children to bed and do the whole bedtime routine! This is assuming you have that kind of relationship. The parent will welcome the respite to be able to do whatever she or he wants!
- Offer to do some house cleaning or laundry while the parent uses this opportunity to take the children to the park, the movies, or any other activity they haven't had time to do together as a family.
- Suggest that they read supportive, encouraging articles or literature on the healing process and the road to recovery from the divorce. This information will help them recognize that others have felt similar and there is an end to the hurt and pain.
- Do something fun with them, and avoid talking about their current situation. They need a healthy, fun time away from the emotional trauma.
- If both individuals happen to be your friends, reassure each of them that in spite of the current, pending divorce, you still value their individual friendships.
- Bring your friend a chocolate treat and enjoy an evening with her while you watch one of her favorite movies. This will surely give your friend a lift!

Elderly

Many of today's elderly have lived from the first automobile days to man living on a space station. They have experienced life from agriculture being the major economic contributor of America's stability and success to the technological stampede and takeover of the information age. Staying current with all these diverse changes and adjustments in their lives contributed to a vast amount of learning and adaptability. These elderly individuals have proven that they are capable and competent in staying equal to or ahead of the times. For many mature individuals, as the years of life lengthen, there is a deep settling in the soul of self-reliance and independence. Years of making decisions, dictating the direction of their lives, rearing children, and experiencing full and responsible careers have all added to this sense of capability. At some point, however, one of life's frustrating ironies rears its head. The irony is this—just as the elderly individual is able to use the wisdom acquired in life in a richer way and finally has a meaningful grasp on what is truly important in this physical world, the body gradually loses ability and strength and begins its decline. I have heard it said that the "golden years are laced with lead." One would wish we could have the body of a twenty-five-year old without losing the wisdom acquired with age!

So it is with the elderly people with whom we come in contact. They may not have pretty, trim, and youthful-looking bodies, but in many ways they still feel young inside and want to relate to younger generations. Perhaps they don't see as well, or perhaps they have difficulty hearing. Maybe they talk more slowly than is comfortable for you in listening. Generally, they will walk more slowly than you do. Whatever the physical impairment, remember never to be dismissive of them! They would love to be able to have full function of their bodies. After years of self-reliance and independence, it is difficult for them to feel comfortable accepting help from others. Most elderly people do not want to ask for help even when they know they now need it. Be polite and courteous to them. Show respect and be solicitous to them because they are your elders.

Remember a couple of things to keep in mind as you offer your assistance to a senior citizen. First, it is crucial to fairly, accurately assess his or her needs. There is a fine line here. You may think that they are not as strong as they should be to accomplish a task. The inclination then is to overdo making it easier for them. This is not necessarily in their best interests. It takes away the opportunity for them to retain a needed degree of independence.

Secondly, reassess their needs. For example, if the individual is sick and unable to drive, arrange for this service as needed. If the individual gets better, but is frailer, it might be in their best interest to encourage and teach them how to take a bus, if appropriate. Developing new skills and abilities preserves a person's dignity during this transitory period.

Remember that each individual is an incredible person! You may not agree with each person's reasoning or philosophies. You may even dislike some individual's firmly held positions regarding politics, religion, or any of many other attitudes and beliefs gleaned over a lifetime; but nevertheless, each one of these elderly persons is someone worthy to be served. Serve them now, as you would like to be served when you grow old. Below are some examples of giving service to the elderly:

- Offer your time to listen to their history. Ask about their family, their friends, and their work experiences.
- Record their history on tape. Ask them questions about:
  o Their ancestry.
  o Current information and stories about themselves, their spouse, and their children.
  o Memorable work experiences.
  o How they handled some of life's common challenges.
  o Lessons they have learned about living.
- Have a sincere servant's heart! It is vital in offering your help.
- Vacuum their cars or home. (Bending and maneuvering such equipment may be difficult for them.)
- Assist with appropriate outdoor chores, such as shoveling snow, tidying the garden area, and taking out/in garbage bins.
- Offer to drive them to their appointments, or to do necessary or fun shopping with them.
- Offer to clean their floors, dust their furniture, etc., depending, of course, on their living arrangements.
- Decorate their rooms as the season's change, if they are in assisted-living or nursing home situations.

- Offer to give them a ride to one of their favorite places, such as a park, the zoo, the beach, the mountains or an ornamental garden.

- Invite them to your house for an hour or so to give them the opportunity to be around the energy of children. They may enjoy reading to your children or maybe they would prefer to be an observer. If they have no family close, they need other company, and mothers, now elderly, miss the energy and excitement of children.

- Invite them to go to the park with you and your children so that they can delight in observing children at play. Pack an extra sandwich and have them bring one of their food specialties if they would like to do so.

- Shop for their groceries if needed. Make it an occasion the elderly can count on.

- Respect and acknowledge them.

- Bring live music into their homes. Hold a small musical event that won't weary them, but will give them a boost, while sharing your musical talent and/or that of your family.

- Assess their talents. If they have talents that could be used in the community, encourage them, and set up a network for sharing their gifts. If they have products that could be sold, encourage them to continue to produce them, while you find a source to sell them.

- Help with their funeral plans if appropriate. Carry out the plans, as they have desired, if it is appropriate for you to be that involved.
- Celebrate their birthdays with them. You could have a simple cake and card party, or more elaborate plans with invited guests.
- Assess their diets. Often they lose interest in eating properly. Make sure they have access to quality, balanced, and healthy foods. Also, bring in help to cook for them as needed.
- Help them to organize their important papers so that they are readily accessible when needed. One such important paper is a one-page medical reference sheet containing all medications, allergic reactions, a brief summary of medical history with dates, primary doctors, other contracts, and insurance information. This information, along with a copy of a living will and medical treatment plan, should be kept together and quickly accessible in case of a medical emergency.
- Make sure they have a current blood-pressure record when health problems are a constant reality.
- If diabetes is a factor, know where their daily records of blood sugar and insulin amounts are kept. Be capable of drawing the proper insulin dosage and administering the shot. Be sure to have their written permission and consent and their doctor's approval, if needed. If you are not certain about how to do this procedure, make sure you know someone who does that can be

readily available if the elderly individual cannot administer this need himself or herself.

- Keep a record of their appointments handy on a calendar.

- Keep such information as family members' names, birthdays, addresses, and phone numbers together in an easily accessible place. This will assist them in making contacts, sending birthday cards, and sending letters or other communications as desired or needed.

- Maintain regular care of the elderly person's computer (if the elderly person has and is able to use one), with timely internal cleanup of the hard drive so that it is reliable.

- Arrange and have family members rotate weeks of visits, with activities, talent programs, show and tell, or reading to them to help maintain their spirits.

- Consider devices that can be installed to mitigate the difficulty with some of the physical activities that the elderly may be experiencing. For example, if the elderly are capable of living on their own but have difficulty with strength, balance, navigating stairs, and any other such up and down situations, consider installing handles or bars of some kind in areas such as bathrooms, garage areas, stairs, and any other place in the house that would be helpful. Also consider such helps as a seat within a shower stall with a showerhead that adjusts for sitting,

- Bring them a chocolate treat and with them watch one of their favorite movies! Of course, that is if they like chocolate and watching movies!

Empty Nest

Don't get me wrong. As a parent, you have known and wanted the end result to be exactly this—an empty nest. Your job has been to raise your children to be strong, civic minded, courteous, kind, independent, and capable individuals who know how to tackle life on their own. However—Ugh! The anticipation of an empty nest creates a hole in your heart that looms large and feels like it may never mend. As a mother, it feels as if you are being stripped of your feathers when your children take flight from the nest you have built for them. For years we have gathered our chicks under our wings, and fluffed our feathers in satisfaction, knowing that everyone is under our protection and care within that nest.

Then the day comes when the first child takes flight. It is a horrible feeling. You cannot fluff your feathers and know you are protecting them anymore. What is worse is that the next child is standing on the edge of the nest flapping its wings, testing the air currents, and developing strength for its own flight of freedom. Ugh, again! The pattern continues until all the chicks are gone. You are left with an empty nest. This is my experience.

A girlfriend of mine had just the opposite experience. It was a complete surprise to her! She thought she would have that hole-in-the-heart experience that I feel. She did not, to her delight! When her children were on their own, she realized that she was not worrying about them in the same way as before. She knew they were in colleges that they enjoyed. She felt they were grappling with their lives in mature and wonderful ways. She was no longer involved in their day-to-day, hour-by-hour activities, and therefore did not find herself consumed with "Are they going to be home at the appointed hour?" or "When they get home, how many friends are coming with them?" She experienced a sense of freedom that she had not known in years, and a mental burden had been lifted. The energy and mood of the home settled down. This contributed to calming down her soul. It was a wonderfully surprising gift.

Not everyone who experiences the empty nest syndrome gets that gift. Some parents have a real struggle with the whole reality of not having young energy flying in the door at any time, disrupting the home with all the hustle and bustle, and flying back out on a whim! It may be too quiet for their natures. These parents may find your attention to their loneliness very gratifying. A little support and encouragement, from friends, loved ones, and neighbors who have emptied nests of their own, is a wonderful boon. The following thoughtful acts help begin the process of mending "the hole." For those parents who love the new freedom, enjoy your time with new and old friends in a million wonderful ways!

- Present a gift basket or bag with a box of tissues (for dad) and a large, chocolate candy bar (for mom.)

- Create a small nest using a colorful bucket with straw or other material resembling a bird's nest. Fill the bucket with fun personally appropriate gift items.

- Take the parent(s) out for lunch or dinner and ask questions about their now grown up children. Be interested in their activities. Let the parents talk.
- Encourage the parent(s) to develop personal interests that have lain dormant for years.
- Suggest to the parent(s) that they consider serving a humanitarian mission of some kind, if funds, health, and time allow.
- Suggest community service if it would better suit their time and talents.
- Suggest going back to college as an option if the parents have not finished their education and an interest remains, or even if a new educational interest would sound fulfilling to them.
- Encourage them to volunteer at local schools.
- Suggest sharing of parent's knowledge, specialty, talent, or a service that he or she would enjoy doing. Such a service might be one on a voluntary basis or taught in a school or community at a reduced rate of recompense.
- Invite these people to share an impromptu outing with you. The break in their routine is refreshing.
- Hold a monthly "empty nesters" get-together.
- Suggest they adopt another child when none of the above suggestions help. (Just kidding!)
- Share a delicious chocolate treat and enjoy a warm, humorous movie together!

Funeral

This is a tough day for the family. Be sensitive about the timing of your visits. The family may not have the energy or inclination to interact with those outside of immediate family and close friends. Preparing for the funeral is considerable effort, which needs focused attention, and it perpetuates the emotionally draining experiences that come with their recent loss. (A word to the family whose loved one died—allow people to help you in ways that may be of service to you!) The following suggestions will help you know what is appropriate service for this tender, sacred, and painful time.

- If you are at a loss as to what to do, call the person in charge and offer your help for whatever is needed.

- Offer to greet the family and friends that come to the funeral home and to direct them, if needed.

- Volunteer to stay in their home during the viewing and funeral. (There are people who take advantage of the family's absence during the funeral service and will rob the home.)

- For funeral services held out of town, consider the following ideas:
    - Put together an age-appropriate travel kit for the children. Paper, pencils, granola, color crayons, fast-food gift certificates, tissues, raisins, etc.
    - Offer to bring age-appropriate books on tape.

Do Something! Specific Ideas for Specific Situations

- Offer to collect the mail, water their lawn, change lights, take the garbage in and out, park your car in their driveway, or get the newspaper.
- Wash the family's car so that it is clean if it is needed during this time. Also, it is especially considerate to fill it up with gasoline.
- Offer to get the children's shoes and clothes ready for the funeral service.
- Send the family a box of thank-you cards and postage stamps to help them with their responses. Funeral homes usually do not give them enough.
- Donate enough paper or plastic products, such as dishes, utensils, and napkins to last a week or so for the stream of visitors that they may have following the funeral.
- Prepare for freezer storage any surplus food items that have been brought to the home. These foods may be very helpful at a later time.
- Help set up the meal for the family members after the funeral services.
- At the family meal following the funeral services, arrange the donated flowers and plants in an attractive manner.
- Take the flowers, plants, and other mementos of remembrance that were used at the funeral service to the family home when the service is completed.
- Do not stop being a friend after the intensity dies

- down. Stay in contact with the family and keep offering your love and support.
- Lovingly and tactfully contact the family if you notice significantly changed behavior in your mourning friend weeks or months after the event. If you are close enough to the family and they have not been physically near enough to notice such changes, tell them of your concerns in case professional counseling may be needed.
- Eventually, a chocolate treat and a warm, humorous movie will feel okay. (This must be a time-sensitive offering!)

Hospitalization, Illness and Operation

Thank goodness for the medical facilities and knowledge that is available for those who need that expertise! That being said, the hospital is not the place anyone wants to stay. It is loud, noisy, uncomfortable, smelly, and full of strange viruses and bacteria. The patient rarely gets a good nights rest, and it is not uncommon that the patient hurts—a lot.

Be sensitive to time your visits according to the patient's comfort level. This is important. If you stop by the hospital without previous notice, make sure that your visit is not intruding on private family time, or is not delaying medical procedures or attention. It is best to keep your visits short. Whatever service you decide to give, it is always appreciated. The following are suggestions for serving the patient:

- Bring any of the following items:
  - Age-appropriate books on tape.
  - Peaceful and relaxing music.
  - A fluffy and soft animal to hold.
  - A small, soft, fuzzy quilt, or lap blanket.
  - Flowers (they always bring cheer.)
  - A potted plant in a pretty container.
  - A balloon bouquet. Note: latex balloons are not allowed in the hospital. Mylar balloons are acceptable. (Save the latex balloons for when the patient is at home.)
  - Special drinks, candy, or healthy snacks.
  - Personal photos of animals, family, or friends of patient.
  - New, soft pajamas, slippers, or fashion socks.
  - Bath gift-set or personal cleaners and moisturizers.
  - Attractive hair accessories.
  - Useful toiletries.
- Be a source of help for a woman patient's concern about her appearance. This help is especially important if she must be hospitalized for a lengthy period of time. All women would agree that hair that is greasy or unkempt is depressing. Consider shampooing your friend's hair with waterless shampoo. Better still, if you have the facilities and approval of the nursing staff, shampoo with water.

- Be ready with a bowl, shampoo, towel, and hair dryer. This most welcome service will make all the difference in your friend's state of mind!
- Consider offering make-up for a woman if she has an extended stay. Also bring a new and attractive outfit for her to wear. This will contribute to bolstering her spirits.
- Offer her some fun interactive entertainment if she is to be hospitalized for more than a few days. Consider the following:
  - Play fun and relaxing board games or brainteasers.
  - Consider reading to the patient when he or she doesn't have the strength or ability to read, but is attentive and mentally alert.
  - You could read uplifting magazine articles, short stories, novels, religious texts such as the Bible or other personal choices, or biographies.
  - Share crossword, or other word puzzles.
- Spread your visits throughout the week, instead of making Sunday the only day you visit. Many people make their visits on that day and weary the patient.
- Share your gift of music if you have a musical talent that can be offered in the patient's area—for the enjoyment of your friend and other patients nearby. Always get prior permission from the staff and perhaps check with the family of the patient as well. (It could be voice, flute, violin, cello, accordion and so forth.)

- Bring a special food treat. For example, one woman was brought a strawberry milk shake after weeks in the hospital. She remembers it tasting so delicious. It brought a welcome change from hospital food. (Of course bringing such treats is with the assurance that the patient is not on a special diet.)

- Buy gift certificates to book stores, video stores, or convenience stores for future needs or wants.

- Any homemade treat such as sweet rolls, breads, cookies, or caramel popcorn, is always welcome.

- When you visit, let the patient know you are willing to listen to anything they may want to talk about. Sometimes they just want to complain about the situation, the food, the facilities, or the nursing staff. Let them complain and be allowed to express any frustration they may feel.

- Prearrange a visit from one of the patient's favorite people, such as a schoolteacher, music teacher, or mentor.

- If they agree, take pictures of the progress and recovery of the patient. Present the patient with a photo album of these pictures after his or her release from the hospital. Including pictures of their favorite medical staff would be a nice reminder of that experience.

- Buy a new shirt or sweater for a gentleman whose hospital stay is extended.

- Consider a hand and arm or foot and lower leg massage if the patient is in a physical condition to tolerate some touching and it isn't medically contra-indicated.
- Remember that men have a hard time sitting in the hospital. They need visitors also, and find relaxation with a trusted friend who stops by to buoy their spirits.
- Put a poster up and have all the visitors sign it.
- Make a poster with get-well wishes of those who are not able to make it to the hospital.

Aside from the patient, many other people are affected and may be worn out. Here are some services you could provide to the doctors, nursing staff, or family:

- The medical staff always appreciates a sincere and heartfelt note of thanks for their attentions and careful nursing. These notes often are sent to the administrators of the hospital and they receive welcome recognition from their superiors.
- Bring a healthy snack or fun gifts to the nursing staff that is tending the patient.
- Volunteer to sit with the family in the lounge to keep them company if the patient is in the ICU. Be sure there is always someone with the family in the beginning stages of the experience.
- Ask a family member if they would like you to notify their spiritual/religious leader. Offer to take this individual to the hospital as needed.
- Bring a basket of healthy food and enjoyable magazines.

- For extended family stays, consider the following ideas:
  - Bring dinner to them on occasion.
  - Consider bringing a cooler of food that can be used and refilled with the family's favorite treats or foods to sustain them during the long hours of bedside waiting.
  - Help to maintain the outside appearance of their home if the stay is extended, or if the person is having alternative treatments out of town. This gives the appearance of occupancy and discourages any mischief from outsiders. It also helps maintain an attractive appearance of the home in keeping with the rest of the neighborhood.
  - With their permission, do the family laundry while they are away.
  - Offer to take care of their pet or pets as needed.
- Supply a notebook or journal to write down the names of visitors. Often visitors come when the patient is in a drugged stupor and unable to know or remember who visited.
- Offering personal messages of love are always welcome and can come in many forms. One family wrote a poem about their visit and gave it as a gift to the patient.
- Relieve the family from the long hours of sitting and waiting. Encourage them to leave the hospital

for a while as you sit with the patient in their absence.

- Use your time, if the patient is sleeping while you are relieving the family, to get some of your own quiet projects done, such as, reading, journal writing, handwork, or homework.

- Leave a thoughtful and inspiring message on the answering machine at home for the family to listen to when they return.

- Consider taking into your home other children still at home while the parents and/or child are in the hospital, or (with the parent's permission) provide a live-in caregiver until the parents return.

- Give some money to the teenager siblings of a patient to go to dinner and a movie. The remaining children of the family feel forgotten or shuffled aside when their sibling is in the hospital getting all the attention.

- Loan your cell phone for the parents' use if they don't have one. (Note: cell phones are to be used only outside of hospitals.)

- Bring a delicious chocolate treat (maybe a decadent old-fashioned milk shake) and an uplifting and humorous movie when it is appropriate!

Homebound or Shut-in

People may be homebound for a variety of reasons and sometimes for an extended period of time. They may not be sick, but may be dealing with any of a myriad of physically restricting problems like a bad knee, hip, or back. Thus they may choose to remain in the confines of their homes, perhaps needing the assistance of moving about with a wheelchair or walker. There are other rare but real problems such as agoraphobia, a condition in which the person battles real fear based issues.

Acts of kindness that can be offered to the house bound person helps promote the feeling "someone cares about and remembers me," and considers them a viable, valuable part of the community. The following ideas can help them feel of your concern:

- Bring ability-appropriate service projects for them to do, such as tying a quilt or assembling school kits or emergency kits. (Provide the items for the kits, with instructions.)

- Direct this homebound individual into sharing his or her talents, such as woodcrafting, crocheting, or scrapbooking. Try to match a service that is needed in your community with this person's talents, and offer guidance in using and/or further developing this skill. For example, crocheting leper bandages would be very useful. Another suggestion might be to knit hot pads, dish clothes, or other such items for someone else who is in need of a "gift of lift." Provide the supplies and return to pick up the finished projects.

- Consider the following:

- o Play fun and relaxing board games or brainteasers.
- o Read uplifting magazine articles, short stories, novels, scriptures, or biographies aloud.
- o Share crossword, or other word puzzles.
- o Teach them skills that are appropriate for their condition, such as crocheting, knitting, or painting.

- Have them teach you one of their skills if they are physically able and appear eager to do so.
- Bring them books on tape from the library. Assess their interests and offer to keep them supplied as long as they are wanted.
- Give this person a gift certificate for an online bookstore and/or video store.
- Bring amusing audiotapes, DVD, or CD that are adapted to their sense of humor. (For example, Garrison Keillor, Jerry Seinfeld, Johnny Carson, *The Honeymooners, I Love Lucy,* etc.)
- Consider what one family did in the case of a temporarily homebound friend. This family put a bed in the living room and made that the center of activity. When meals were brought in, the children "camped out" with mom.
- Buy them a phone card so that they can stay in touch with long distance friends and family.
- Offer to shop for their ongoing grocery needs.
- Pick up medications as needed.

- Maintain their yard, or for a long-term situation, enlist and coordinate help on a rotating basis.
- Be prepared to do light house-cleaning when necessary. Be certain this person is comfortable and accepting of this help. Be respectful of specific ways that that person wants any such cleaning done.
- Buy a couple of month's worth of professional cleaning services for them.
- Do some of the laundry, with their approval. You may find this a task you can do as you are visiting. You may even decide to offer to do this on a weekly schedule, time and conditions permitting.
- Organize meals to be brought in if they can't physically keep up with the cooking. Use willing neighbors to bring in food or consider soliciting the services of community resources such as Meals on Wheels.
- Consider offering a hand and arm massage, or a foot and lower leg massage.
- Consider the person's concern for his or her animals. Offer to take them on walks, or if necessary, to a groomer or veterinarian appointment.
- Water the indoor plants as needed.
- With the individuals approval, offer to clean and organize the pantry. Throw out old and forgotten items that create clutter and are not used. Reline the shelves with new paper.
- Consider giving them a manicure or pedicure,

or arrange for and pay for this service.

- Shampoo the person's hair. If needed, set, perm, or color it if you know how. If not, arrange for someone to come in who does have that expertise. For men, offer to wash and/or trim their hair, or arrange to have it done.
- With the individuals approval, consider the following house hold chores:
  - Change the linens on the beds.
  - Clean the carpets occasionally.
  - Wash the windows as needed.
  - Vacuum and dust as needed. See that this service gets done on a timely basis. (Consider enlisting young adults to take care of this on a regular schedule.)
- Remember to bring a delicious chocolate treat and offer to watch an uplifting, humorous movie with them—with or without the family!

Infertility

Many of us assume that when we want to build a family it will happen just as nature intended. A human egg is fertilized with a human sperm, through intercourse, and *voila!* Nine months later a human baby is born. Obviously, this doesn't work for everyone. One or both parents may not be capable of contributing what is necessary to create this miracle. Sometimes there simply is not a medically known reason for conception not occurring.

It can be a shattering emotional experience when a

couple is informed that they are infertile. The dream and hope of having a biological child of their own has been dramatically compromised. At this point, the uncertainty of whether or not they will ever experience parenthood feels like a dark, looming cloud that overshadows other possible parenting options. The couple feels insecure, anxious, and unsure regarding the parenting path with which they are now faced. It is so different from what they had imagined they would experience.

The emotional transition of accepting this new reality is different for each individual. Sometimes one or the other partner never accepts their situation. At other times, a couple eventually comes to accept their infertile state and be emotionally united and ready to move forward together. Despite emotional differences that occur regarding their infertility, at some point couples may consider several parenting alternatives. Common family-building options include adoption, using a surrogate mother, or in vitro fertilization. I have chosen to highlight in vitro fertilization in this section.

Statistics show that 6.1 million Americans are infertile. That being the case, there is a vast amount of information on infertility. There were many enlightening resources I found in researching this topic. One organization called Resolve, the National Infertility Association, stated the following: "One of the most challenging aspects of the infertility experience is dealing with the emotional ups and downs relating to medical treatment, the uncertainty about outcomes, and the challenge of having to make important decisions such as when 'enough is enough.' It is important to learn how to take care of yourself, to make sure you get the support you need, and to manage your emotions so that your self-esteem and outlook on life remains as positive as possible".[4]

Many wonderful books have been written on infertility. The available resources are too numerous to mention here. However, I would encourage anyone who wants to broaden their understanding of this pain-filled reality, to use the numerous and helpful support systems that are accessible in libraries, bookstores, the Internet, magazine publications, and support groups.

Because in vitro fertilization is a complicated, stressful, and difficult experience for the woman physically, mentally, and emotionally, the following suggestions may bring some comfort to her. These suggestions came from women who have experienced infertility and undergone the in vitro process.

- Find a doctor and a fertility center with which you can connect emotionally. A medical staff that you feel shares a similar philosophy and outlook regarding fertility is extremely important. The medical staff should express sensitivity to your emotions, answer your questions thoroughly and recognize and sympathize with your pain. These are valid expectations.

- Be your own advocate. If you and/or your partner have reservations, boldly ask unanswered questions or state clearly your hesitancies until you are satisfied with the answers.

- Establish a respectful and mature relationship with your doctor.

- Get counseling or other help you may need if you

---

4. http://www.resolve.org

are having a difficult time accepting the fact that other people have babies while you have not been so blessed. Inevitably, you will have to come in contact with other people's babies. It is vital to finally be able to face this reality without falling apart whenever you say the word "baby."

- Recognize that the drugs you need for fertility will break you down emotionally. Establish a safe network of family and friends who will respond to your physical and emotional needs.

- Discuss your infertility with family or friends. It is important that you feel emotionally safe with them, as this is a very sensitive and raw subject for you. Avoid situations which may invite insensitive questions and remarks.

- Consider joining a support group. Check with your fertility clinic for reputable groups.

- Realize that it's not the end of the world if the fertility procedures don't succeed.

- Count what blessings you do have.

- Continue to do simple things that give you pleasure which help to balance you emotionally. The following examples are from the American Fertility Association:
  o Put flowers on your desk or at home.
  o Get a massage or a pedicure.
  o Go to a movie of your choice.
  o Go to the theater. Something comical helps to

lighten the mood.

- o Keep involved with any kind of physical activity that you find satisfying. If weight gain is a problem, exercise will give you some measure of control over your body.
- o Learn relaxation techniques. Deep breathing, visualization, meditation, and muscle relaxation are all great ways to calm your spirit and psyche. These disciplines will also benefit your daily life on many levels.
- o Consider doing volunteer work. Serving others always makes our own problems seem less tragic.
- o Consider seeing an infertility counselor or therapist if you feel your emotions are extreme and out of control.[5]

It's important to take care of yourself through trials like this. Still, help from a solid support system can make a world of difference. Following are suggestions for those who give support:

- Listen with an empathic ear. Allow your suffering friend or relative to discuss all the feelings she has at the moment. See chapter five.
- Make sure she understands that you will be there for her whenever she has a need to talk. If there is a scheduling conflict, reschedule as soon as possible.

---

5. http://www.theafa.org

- Be sensitive to her ability to cope with discussing the "baby" topic. If she were still in an emotionally tender place, it would be better not to invite her to functions that revolve around babies such as births and baby showers.
- Refer to ideas that are listed in chapter six.
- Focus on a particular interest of hers and suggest that you pursue this interest together.
- Offer a spa treatment such as a pedicure, massage, or facial.
- Give her a hug and let her cry.

Remember the importance of words. The following phrases are never helpful:

"Relax; it's all in your head. Take a vacation. Then you'll get pregnant."

"Don't worry so much. It just takes time. You'll get pregnant if you're just patient."

"If you adopt a baby, you'll get pregnant."

- And if you can't think of anything else, bring her a delicious chocolate treat and watch a warm, humorous movie together!

Long Term Care/Disabilities

Long-term care is categorically well termed as a "Garden trial or Garden service." It could involve weeks, months, and sometimes years of service from the family and close, dedicated friends. This service goes far beyond dropping off a plate of cookies with a note of love and encouragement. Long-term care requires patience and a real sacrifice of time.

It may be inconvenient for the helper. The follow through of promises of care or the fulfilling of the family or patient's expectations is vital. Follow-up care is also extremely important. Each act of remembrance and support, such as the ones listed, is greatly valued.

- As with any illness, establish and maintain a trusting relationship. This may involve a testing period. The receiver may suggest small needs at first to determine if, in fact, the one serving will follow through. It is disappointing and disheartening to depend on a person for a needful act only to realize that nothing will actually get done.
- Consider the ideas previously mentioned:
    o Play fun and relaxing board games or brainteasers.
    o Read uplifting magazine articles, short stories, novels, scriptures, or biographies aloud.
    o Share crossword or other puzzles.
    o Teach them skills that are appropriate for their condition: perhaps crocheting, knitting, or painting, etc.
- Care or arrange care for the disabled person in a way that permits the family to attend Sunday services on a regular basis if possible, and occasionally, if not. Being responsible for round-the-clock care, the family would benefit greatly from such a generous and thoughtful gesture. If the disabled person is able to attend church

services but his disability requires special care or is distracting to others, perhaps walking the halls or keeping him or her appropriately cared for while the meeting is in progress would be a welcome service.

- Lend a listening ear! See chapter five. Sometimes the family can be overwhelmed or frustrated by the nonstop schedule of a disabled loved one. This should not be taken as a sign that they don't want to care for the person! It was suggested to me that one should not recommend that the disabled person be placed in a home for the disabled. Allow the family to safely express their frustration. Advice is not required and not appreciated. It is recommended that you listen, and try to be clear about the emotions, thoughts, and feelings of the family. Sometimes the family members just want to vent.

- Be a secret pal to the disabled for a while. Drop off goodies, small gifts, and notes of encouragement. One family experienced this with their paraplegic son. He received weekly surprises and would grin with anticipation every time the doorbell would ring. Knowing someone out there cared for him helped ease his depression and brought him much needed joy. (The mother who encouraged this service enlisted the help of her teenage sons to drop off the weekly gifts. They were being taught the value of serving others and the satisfaction that comes with anonymous giving.)

- Make sure you follow up on offers to help.
- Offer to take care of a pet or pet's needs, which may include veterinarian and/or grooming appointments.
- Encourage the family not to be afraid to ask for any kind of help that is needed.
- Offer to help with housekeeping chores. If you are financially able, pay for a couple of months of professional cleaning services.
- One family I talked with has a twenty-year-old daughter with the mental ability of a five-year-old child. The daughter thinks that she does not need to be involved in activities and programs geared to her mental capabilities. She therefore spends most of her time at home with her parents. This is taxing on her mother, who has seven other children and is also heavily involved in her husband's business. This mother's advice to those who want to be of service in this kind of situation is for friends or neighbors to offer to include the mentally handicapped person in some of their own activities. This could include shopping, going to a movie, or other appropriate activities that keep the son or daughter occupied, interested in life, and not underfoot when other pressing family matters need to be handled.
- Value the person. Treat him or her with the respect you would give a fully functioning friend.

- Engage in meaningful conversation. Ask questions, with genuine interest, that will allow you to get to know the person better. Resist the tendency to talk condescendingly, more slowly, or more loudly.
- Offer to spend quality one-on-one time with this individual. This will help the person with disabilities to feel less lonely, and it will give you the chance to discover personality traits and talents of this person that might not be noticeable within group settings.
- Be willing to share things about yourself. Let them get to know you too. It is just as important as you getting to know them.
- Consider offering a hand and/or arm massage. Maybe a foot and/or lower leg massage would be appreciated as well.
- Show love with action. Do little things—a smile, a note, a telephone call. Or, extend an invitation to a luncheon, a party, or an evening event. These can make all the difference in their ability to persevere in their affliction.
- If you are unsure about the condition of the individual, ask direct and clear questions about the disability. This understanding will help you know how to better serve this unique individual.
- Consider sewing theme pillow-covers for the seat cushion of a wheelchair that is used regularly.

- Invite the disabled person to go to parties with you, or visit another person who needs comfort. Be available or arrange for the needed transportation. Remember to take them home before they get too tired, even if the activity is not over.
- Encourage a young man or young woman to help prepare clothing, dress, and transport the disabled person to meetings, appointments, or other activities.
- Offer to give the parents of a disabled person a night out. This loving service is especially helpful during the holidays.
- Get creative and bring a chocolate treat to eat and a warm, humorous movie for them to watch! (This could be very helpful for the primary caregiver!)

Miscarriage

A miscarriage of an acknowledged pregnancy is a very sad event for a woman. The woman who has experienced it seldom discloses it. The quiet loss is poignant and painful, accompanied by heart-wrenching emotions. Often her partner shares these heavy-hearted feelings as well.

According to the March of Dimes a miscarriage is defined as, "a pregnancy loss that occurs before 20 weeks, before the fetus is able to survive outside the womb. Most miscarriages occur in the first trimester or 12 weeks of pregnancy. A miscarriage can be an intensely sad and frightening experience. A pregnancy that had seemed normal suddenly ends, leaving expectant parents devastated. About 15 percent of recognized pregnancies end this way."[6]

A friend of mine described it as a "loss of a dream." That description aptly described the common explanations I heard from many women I questioned regarding miscarriages that they had experienced. With joyful expectation, recognizing that a lovely, warm bundle was growing inside of her, the woman forms a bond with the fetus early in pregnancy. This bond develops each day, and often the mother naturally anticipates the child's future and all the wonderful interactions she is going to have. She may even give the fetus a nickname, which she and her partner playfully refer to during the ensuing months of growth. She expects an armful of soft, responsive warmth to nurture and cuddle at the end of gestation. Suddenly, it's over! The dream, the hope, has been shattered.

I recall a very good friend of mine who miscarried at about four months. She collected the fetus in a plastic bag as the doctor had instructed. Before she went to her appointment, she showed it to me. As I looked upon this very miniscule human body, I realized the importance of this fetus to my friend. She had named her, she had often talked about her, and she deeply mourned her loss. I remember feeling inadequate in knowing how to comfort her.

"HopeXchange" is an organization of women in New Zealand that sponsors and supports other women who have experienced miscarriages. They know what they are talking about. The founders and contributors of this Web site have experienced this grievous personal loss. It is full of valuable

---

[6]. http://www.marchofdimes.com

information for the woman suffering this loss and for those who want to give comfort and support. For more detailed information or to have your questions answered more thoroughly, I refer you to their Web site at www.hopexhange.com. The following information is taken directly from their website, with their permission.

"The Grief Process: What should I expect?

The grieving process involves three steps:

Step 1: Shock/Denial: "This really isn't happening. I've been taking good care of myself."

Step 2: Anger/Guilt/Depression: "Why me? If I would have . . . " "I've always wanted a baby so badly, this isn't fair. I feel more sadness in my life now more then ever."

Step 3: Acceptance: "I have to deal with it. I'm not the only one who has experienced this. Other women have made it through this, maybe I should get some help."

"Each step takes longer to go through than the previous one. There are unexpected and sometimes-anticipated triggers that lead to setbacks. Examples of potential triggers include: baby showers, birth experience stories, new babies, OB/GYN office visits, nursing mothers, thoughtless comments, holidays, and family reunions.

"When we offer help to someone through this time, they are often in such shock they don't know what they need.

The objectives are to encourage the venting of her grief and reestablishing her self-esteem while recognizing her sorrow. Whatever the person is feeling, they deserve to have their feelings supported by the people around them." The following suggestions from HopeXchange are particularly helpful:

- "Contact is important. Be there if possible, but if not, ring or write.
- A hug or arm around her shoulders is comforting.
- Understand that her tears are a healthy response and should never be discouraged. Having a box of tissues handy is helpful.
- Let her do the talking. Be the passive partner who asks questions and focus on certain points to help her talk about her feelings. It is sufficient to just listen.
- Tell her how you feel about her losing the baby and how sorry you are.
- Acknowledge her pain even if you think you would not react this way in this situation.
- Ask questions about her experience, how she is really feeling and what she is thinking about.
- Encourage her to be patient and not to impose 'shoulds' on herself. Grieving takes time.
- Reassure them they did everything they could and it wasn't their fault. It helps alleviate their guilt.
- Grieving is a physically exhausting process and she will probably need to sleep or rest during the

- day. Take whatever steps necessary to give her the uninterrupted peace to do this.
- The intensity of grief fluctuates. During less tearful times a change of scenery is appreciated.
- Do something practical such as shopping or taking around a meal.
- Put on soothing music for her to listen to, offer a back massage, a walk on the beach. When she feels ready, take her to a movie of her choice.
- If you are seriously worried about her behavior, seek professional advice. As a rule of thumb, as long as she is not damaging herself, another person or property, you probably don't have anything to worry about."

Refer to chapter six for many other positive suggestions to support and comfort. As always, along with the many ways you can help, be sure to avoid the following hurtful actions:

- "Don't ignore her because you feel helpless or uncomfortable with grief. She will wonder if what happened to her means nothing to you.
- Don't think that miscarriage is easier to cope with than a stillbirth or neonatal death. The truth is that her baby has just died, and it doesn't really matter how pregnant she was.
- Don't be anxious or embarrassed about making her cry. It is not what you said or did that upset her, but losing the baby. By allowing her to cry, you are helping her work through the process of grief.

- Don't confuse support with "cheering her up." Grief is an enormously powerful emotion and needs releasing, not repressing.
- Don't put on a bright cheery front yourself.
- Don't assume there will be another pregnancy.
- Don't try to do all the housework. Although your intentions are good, allowing her to do some herself will help her to feel capable and useful.
- Don't forget her children have lost a sibling, and it is natural for them to react in some way.
- Don't feel guilty if you're pregnant. Just forgive her if she's cold and withdrawn, it's her way of coping.
- Don't feel you have to keep your children away. She must go through the process of accepting others' children.
- Don't ask how she is feeling if you only do so as a social obligation. It obliges you to listen carefully to the complete answer.
- Seven Helpful things to say:
    o "I'm so sorry about your miscarriage."
    o "I know how much you wanted that baby."
    o "It's okay to cry."
    o "Can I call you back next week to see how you are doing?"
    o "I was wondering how you are feeling about your miscarriage now?"

-
    - o "I don't really know what to say."
    - o "It must be so awful for you after going through those weeks of IVF treatment to have lost your baby."
- Seven Things NOT to say:
    - o "You can always have another one."
    - o "There was probably something wrong with it. It's nature's way."
    - o "It's God's will."
    - o "At least you didn't know the baby. It would have been much worse if it had happened later."
    - o "I know how you feel."
    - o "It wasn't really a baby yet."
    - o "You're young, there's plenty of time. If you stop focusing on being pregnant so much it will just happen."
- *If in doubt, say something—anything—and be prepared to listen. Possibly the hardest thing, even harder than hearing an insensitive comment, is when people say nothing at all."*[7]
- Bring your friend a delicious chocolate treat and share a warm, humorous girl movie together, as soon as you feel it is appropriate!

---

7. http://www.hopexchange.com

Moving Day

Has any one not experienced a move? Yuck! Even though this list is a bit short, because we all have gone through this difficult, wearying, and taxing time, I suspect each of us can come up with one or two ideas that may not be listed here. Personalize your offerings based on what you found to be helpful in your moves. There is no way around it—it is 100 percent physically and emotionally draining. So offer your muscles and a smile. Anything is appreciated!

- One person advised to make sure that the person or family wants help before offering. Some people don't want or need the extra hands.
- Find out specifically what kind of help is needed. Ask directly, look around, see the obvious, and then jump in and do the work.
- Offer to help do some preliminary packing if you know in advance when they are moving. There are numerous miscellaneous items that can be packed well before moving day.
- Offer to help do anything. Bring drinks, tend the children, and if there is enough muscle power, help unpack or pack boxes, set up beds, and so forth.
- Arriving with food is always appreciated. This is especially true if the power has been turned off. If it is summertime, bring cold drinks, sandwiches, and fruit. If it is in the wintertime, hot chocolate and soup are great comfort foods.
- Put new liners in closets, drawers, or the pantry.
- Help collect boxes and packing material before moving day.

- Help move closet clothes by rubber banding the handles of the hangers together (if the move is local.)
- Clean closets/drawers after they are emptied.
- Help clean the house after everything has been moved out.
- Make time, at the end of the day, to share a yummy chocolate treat (hot chocolate in the winter and chocolate ice cream in the summer) and a warm, humorous movie!

New Move, New Area

This category could have been put under "Moving Day," but I felt it needed to be a separate listing. Moving into a new neighborhood, let alone a whole new area where the unfamiliar looms large, is overwhelming to say the least! If someone does not have a network of family or friends in the area, getting settled can be intimidating. Here are some ideas that may help the transition go more smoothly for the family:

- Volunteer (as an individual or as a group) to clean and prepare the house to receive the furniture. This service was done by a group of volunteers for a family with a recently built house. It was a large project! They went in and cleaned up all the construction mess inside the house so the family could bring in their personal effects on a timely schedule. It is a service that is usually paid for, but this group of neighbors wanted to do it without pay and did so in two and a half hours!

- Find out what day the family is moving in and bring in dinner for the first couple of nights.
- Pay an initial visit within a day or two of your new neighbor's arrival. Give them friendly and uplifting information about the area and the neighbors.
- Offer to take them to cultural, community, or church activities until they have met a few people and are comfortable going on their own.
- A homemade loaf of bread with a friendly welcome note is always appreciated. Take along some jam, honey, or butter also.
- Make a list of professionals in the area that are highly recommended. Include doctors, dentists, salons (hair and nails), schools, day care, music teachers, nurseries (for the yard), and numbers of churches. Also helpful are the numbers to city hall, the police, animal services, and other community services.
- Children of a similar age could help make cookies and take a plate over to their new friend.
- Lend extra hands to help move the furniture into the home. Such help is always appreciated.
- Offer to tend the children during moving day.
- Take over food and drinks for the laborers.
- Set up the bed frames first and then put on the bedding.
- Help to unpack and organize the kitchen.

- Bring them a delicious chocolate treat and a warm, humorous movie for them to watch—when the family is all settled!

New Baby—Adoption/Natural

I remember being in a class about motherhood that was taught by a mother of eight. She expressed the idea that the first two weeks of a child's life is the sweetest time for a mother and child to have together. She stated that this was the time when a woman feels as close to heaven as she will ever experience as a woman on earth. I recall understanding and agreeing with this sentiment completely.

There has been nothing in my life to compare with the supreme bliss and contentment of those first couple of weeks. Ah, babies! Dan and I videotaped our children's births, and each time we watch them I am immediately transported back to that day which was filled with wonder, joy, gratitude, and bliss. I am a changed woman forever.

Sometimes there can be physical defects with the baby that may or may not be expected upon delivery. The parent's initial realization of this heartbreaking condition is one of the most difficult with which to cope. One woman said that when she was told her child had PKU, (a disease in which the body is unable to break down and metabolize the amino acid, phenylalanine) she withdrew from social contact. She needed time to cry. It was necessary for her to have space and time to process this change in her circumstances and deal with her grief and pain. She understood people's desires to want to visit with her or assist her as she adjusted to being a new mother. But it was important for her to be in a quiet place with only her baby. Once she felt strong enough to cope with her new realities, she was in a better place emotionally to accept the kindnesses of others. Respecting the privacy of a new mother under any kind of circumstances is thoughtful and welcome.

People can forget that even though a woman has not given birth to a newly adopted child, her needs, as well as the family needs, are similar to mothers who have given birth. Be sensitive to adoption situations and offer to help them with any of the following ideas. Each of the ideas listed below can certainly ease the initial load of any new mother, one who has given birth or one who has an adopted infant or child.

- Always call before stopping by!
- Take a basket of healthy snack foods, a magazine, lotion, powder, lip balm, some calming music, or a favorite drink for the mother.
- Offer to take younger siblings to a park, to your home, or out shopping (if you are brave enough!).
- Offer to take a younger sibling or siblings to your home to play with your children once a week for a couple of hours for a month.
- Bring a humorous book to the new mother.
- Offer to watch the baby as you give the new mother an opportunity to take a much-needed nap.
- Bring her favorite treat.
- Leave your little children at your home when you visit.

- Consider offering a hand and arm massage, or a foot and lower leg massage (as with other categories that center on physical recovery.)
- Bring a meal! They are always appreciated—especially between two and four weeks later. See the section called "Let's Talk Food" in chapter six.
- Send a card or an encouraging note with a fun quote.
- Give a subscription to a diaper service if you are in the financial position. Check with the mother to make sure she wants to use cotton diapers.
- If the above offering is declined, how about giving her a few months worth of housecleaning services.
- If the baby is bottle-fed and your friendship with the mother is one of shared trust and confidence, offer to spend the night and take care of the feeding times, which allows the mother to get at least one full night of sleep!
- Consider offering to run to the store for items she may need.
- Take her out to lunch if she feels that she can get away.
- Plan on spending time just listening–see chapter five.
- Never give advice! (Unless it is asked for.)
- Offer to help with the laundry. It may be greatly appreciated. One new body in the house seems to triple the laundry load. Consider taking it to

your own home to get it done so that you are not underfoot at the new mother's house.

- Offer to do a little house cleaning. Two extra hands are always helpful.
- Pay for a professional house-cleaning service for a month or two, if funds allow.
- Take some time with a new mother and help her with the basics of baby care, if she has no family in the area.
- Check in with a new teenage mom after a couple of weeks and assess her needs. She probably could use a break from the constancy of motherhood, especially since it is so drastic a change from her previous activities.
- Find community resources that would be helpful for young mothers and encourage her to get involved. Go with her to the first few meetings until she feels comfortable with the support group.
- Schedule a Friday evening several weeks after the baby arrives where you will bring in dinner for the husband and wife as a date-night dinner. Arrange for the other children to be tended, have the meal prepared, set the table with china, candles, and nice silverware. Play romantic or quiet music in the background.
- Offer to attend to the mother's civic or church responsibilities for a month or two, until she is feeling more balanced.

- Focus on the mother and her baby for this visit. I strongly suggest that you stay clear of discussing your own birthing experiences or war stories from other women.

"Preemies"

The experience of delivering a premature baby is filled with anxiety, stress, and hand wringing. It is so difficult for the parents to leave their child in the hospital when they want desperately to take their baby home with them! Obviously, if that infant survives and can be taken home, the wait will have been worth all the fretfulness and worry. Perhaps the appreciation of that newborn is even more poignant. Love, support, and encouragement from neighbors, friends, and family are all highly valued by the parents. When the family is again reunited at home, the following ideas can be especially helpful.

- Refer to the category "Hospitalization" for ideas that will help with supporting the family during the baby's initial time in NICU.
- Offer to drive her to the hospital if she is still recovering from a particularly difficult delivery and needs someone to assist her in this way.
- Check in with the husband to assess how best to help him with the household chores or children when his wife is at the hospital. Some men need a lot of help while others are pretty self-sufficient and would prefer taking care of the family on their own.

- Show up and offer to listen. (Refer to chapter five.) This is a very emotional time for the mother. Hormones are raging through the body. She is trying to cope emotionally without her baby at home. She may need to have a sympathetic ear in which to vent, and a strong shoulder on which to cry or laugh.
- Help do some of the housework that is not getting done. Clean up the kitchen, do the laundry, or fold and put away clothes as you can. Vacuum, dust, straighten up clutter, and put toys away. All these are helpful services that will be noticed and appreciated.
- Offer to tend the other children when the mother goes to the hospital to visit or nurse her baby.
- Bring a delicious chocolate treat to share and watch a warm, humorous movie together, when it is appropriate!

Parenting
(Stepparenting, Foster Care, Single Parenting)

I include parenting as one of the service categories because of the many difficult issues that come with being a parent. Extra help or comfort may be very much appreciated at times. Nobody is prepared for being a parent. It does not matter how the children come, whether naturally, through adoption, or marriage.

Parenting is a daunting, overwhelming responsibility that requires attention to detail and growing through numerous changes, all while trying to cope with life. Parenting gets even more complicated when families are blended producing a stepparenting situation. If you are involved in foster care with children who are not your own, or you become a single parent, you find yourself in stressful situations at best! Every parent, in whatever parental situation, will at some point, cry "help!"

It is comforting to know that this club of mothers and fathers is bound together by a clear understanding of just how difficult it is to be a parent, let alone an effective one. Some families have extremely harsh, difficult, and upsetting circumstances that never seem to go away. Other homes have normal day-to-day crises that parents are generally capable of handling. And then there are some homes that hum along as the parents gently oversee their kids with very little "head-butting" between generations. Whichever is the case for you, or those you know, be on the alert to give some stressed-out parent their own version of "time-out."

For stepparenting, refer to chapter six. Many of these ideas are great to implement for an overworked and stressed-out parent in an awkward half role. Those ideas, along with some of the following, can also be extremely helpful for single parents. One single parent inspired me by her service despite a very taxing situation.

I met Helen because she was recommended as a woman who intimately understands service. Helen is seventy-three years old, very young at heart, and a delightful and playful individual. After raising three children of her own, Helen has found herself parenting again, but this time as a single parent. She was widowed for the second time in 2004. She is raising two grandsons, ages five and nine. Besides the fact that they are young and busy as boys will be, the oldest child also has autism, which requires greater attention and time. Helen is also heavily involved in community humanitarian work. This work consumes many hours of labor as she organizes workdays, interfaces with the volunteers, and distributes the kits, quilts, and other goods that are donated and assembled to charitable organizations.

My point in highlighting Helen's situation is that other people's choices can and do affect our reality. Helen did not think she would be a hands-on-parent again at this stage in her life, and she certainly didn't count on being a single parent. She is an inspiration to observe as she continues to be highly involved in her life's passion—serving others, while at the same time being a single parent! Because single parents can be so overwhelmed, they can always use some of the following services:

- Organize a teenage workforce to help with outside yard work as needed.

- Relieve the constancy of someone who is single parenting by helping to tend the children. It could be done on a weekly or monthly basis, or as you have time.

- Have a group of young people come to clean, organize, and put away the toys every once in a while.

- Offer to help with the handyman tasks that go with maintaining a house. Change lights or fix problems with the plumbing, water softener, hot water heater, or shingles on the roof (assuming, the single parent is unfamiliar with these tasks.)

- Offer to clean up the yard. You could mow the lawn, rake leaves, tend to the flowerbeds, or weed.
- Consider washing the windows inside and out a couple of times a year.
- Make a date with your friend who is a single parent and take her to dinner and a movie, or lunch and a matinee. Similarly, go to the theater or a concert.

For foster parents, the strain can be of a different nature. Consider some of the ideas in chapter six. You could try the following:

- Help raise money for the sponsoring family to alleviate financial strains that may occur.
- Shop garage sales and pick up toys for the children or other useful items.
- Help foster parents maintain their yard, repair broken household items, or work on projects around the home.
- Assess any special needs that involve the children. In discovering such needs, connect the family with appropriate support groups or agencies. (See "Long-term Care" for other ideas.)
- Okay, let's hear it for some chocolate treats and a warm, funny movie right about now!

Pet Loss

Pets are often a very large part of a family's or an individual's life. To illustrate this point, recall all the pets that were left behind by their owners in their flight of survival from Hurricane Katrina. There were thousands of pets rescued and placed in shelters waiting to be reclaimed. Many of the owners were heartbroken as they were forced to leave their pet behind. There were many happy stories of reunion that serve to reinforce the fact that pets are a huge part of some people's lives. There are also dozens of stories of extraordinary animals that find their way back to their owners after being abandoned or lost. Heartwarming movies about the love, bond, and experiences between an animal and its' owner usually guarantee tears of satisfaction if the story ends happily, or often tears of sadness as deep feelings of understanding and empathy are felt if the story ends in loss. Either way, animals and their relationship with the human family have a huge impact on one's emotional state. When there is pet-loss, it can be a devastating experience.

Sometimes a pet is the family for an individual. The relationship that is built between a pet and its owner is extremely personal; it is one that is built on love, trust, and companionship. When the animal is suffering physically and all the medical help has run its course, the best thing to do is to relieve the pet's suffering by having it put down. However, this decision is very difficult for the owner to make and to accept, let alone to see through. If the pet's life is taken in an accident, the painful emotional repercussions for the owners are acute.

The following story is a very poignant example of love and loss for one young lady. Kelly was ten when she received

Tyana, a beautiful Paint Horse trained for roping, steering, and jumping competition. Many of the skills required in competition are dangerous, with precise timing expected to enable correct execution of the skills without injury to horse or rider. Kelly and Tyana learned to rely on the intricate timing they developed together. This daily practice of skill execution established a deep relationship of trust and connection between them.

One day after riding Tyana, Kelly brushed her, gave her an apple and said good-bye. That evening Tyana's trainer called with the news that Tyana had died. The horse had experienced extreme colic after eating the apple. Her abdomen had become twisted and then ruptured, causing death within two hours.

Her mother received the news feeling shock and grief, knowing how much Kelly adored this horse. She conveyed the news to Kelly as gently as she could and held her daughter tight. During the next couple of days, she listened to all the grief and pain Kelly was able to express. Once Kelly was feeling strong enough to return to school, she found it difficult to relate to the stories of compassion that her friends shared with her on their loss of their dog or cat. She reasoned a relationship with a dog or cat is nothing like the relationship she had with her horse Tyana. Her experience was much more emotionally shattering because of the depth of their bond that was developed while roping, jumping, and working together everyday. A oneness was developed and a dependency created that she didn't feel her friends could form with a typical domestic dog or cat. It was a very difficult period for Kelly.

Six weeks later Kelly's parents purchased her another horse. Snip, the new horse, was not the same as Tyana, and Kelly had a hard time making an emotional connection with it. However, a relationship was formed with satisfying results, personally and professionally. Throughout the next five years, Kelly won fifteen World Buckles, the Youth World Championship and Hi Point English Championship in 2002 as well as the Number One Youth in the Nation for the Year 2002 on the new horse. Recovery from personal pet loss does happen. The process is slow and painful, and often we don't understand why our beloved animal is gone.

Sometimes the loss of a pet is not death. Perhaps the animal has run away or been stolen. Find out the details and contribute your help if there are solutions to the loss. Many organizations are set up to help retrieve pets that are misplaced or lost during disasters. Consider some of the following suggestions to ease the pet owner's pain:

- A phone call expressing your sympathy is always appreciated.

- Awareness by friends of the ache one suffers at the loss of a beloved pet is important. One woman saw an acquaintance at the veterinarian's office with her cat that needed to be put down. She made a phone call to another friend who was on more familiar terms with this acquaintance and relayed the news of this woman's pet loss. That friend took a plate of cookies and an "I'm thinking of you" visit to the bereaved pet owner.

- Consider donating a small amount of money to the family if they are planning to put a headstone on their pet's grave.

- Offer to drive them to the veterinarian's office if they are going to put their pet down. Or, if they feel they are not emotionally strong enough to take their pet to the veterinarian's office, offer to do so for them.
- Buy a small plant or tree for their yard in remembrance of their pet.
- Give fresh flowers with an uplifting note.
- Take them to lunch and let them talk about their animal. Ask questions about their pet. Take an interest in their answers.
- Visit a pet store or animal section of a department store and find an appropriate wall hanging, plaque, or framed saying that would be a reminder of their pet and of the joy their pet brought to them.
- If you have the inclination and money, consider an ad in a newspaper or trade magazine if the pet was an exceptional animal. As in the case of Kelly and Tyana, her mother paid for a one-page ad in the *Paint Horse Journal* to honor the horse and explain the incident of loss to the people who knew the family, followed Kelly's accomplishments, and were concerned for Kelly.
- Bring a wonderful chocolate treat and spend an evening watching a humorous movie with your friend. (I wouldn't recommend movies like *Old Yeller* or *Where the Red Fern Grows!*)

Recuperating after Surgery, Injury, or Illness

The process after an illness, injury, or surgery is often long, pain filled and lonely. It is a time that requires patience of the giver and the receiver. Sometimes family and friends expect recovery and progress to be faster than it actually is. Clear communication between the patient and their loved ones is important. Being too emotionally sensitive is tempting. For everyone involved, it is best to remember not to take comments and conversations too personally. Feelings can be unintentionally hurt. It is important to remember that careful listening and clear understanding of what a recuperating person needs, wants, or expects be made plain for all parties concerned. Keep these ideas in mind:

- Establish a trusting relationship with the recuperating person over a period of time. This could be seen as a testing period. The receiver may suggest small needs at first to determine if you will in fact follow through.

- Offer to tend the children for a couple of hours once a week, or as you can. If there is a more frequent need, put together a list of individuals that would be willing to help tend at such times. Organize the volunteers into hours and days as needed.

- When you visit, something as simple as fluffing their pillows and straightening the sheets and blankets is helpful.

- Refill their water pitcher with fresh water and ice.
- Bring them healthy snacks that are appropriate for their recommended diets.
- Visit and listen. Remember to keep the visit short and sincere. Refer to chapter five for detailed suggestions on effective listening.
- Visit with the family members of the patient while he or she is napping or otherwise occupied. These family members can feel neglected while serving and tending to the person requiring care.
- Offer your home, if circumstances allow, in situations in which surgery and the recuperation period are more extensive than expected. This may arise if the patient's family is unable to house him or the patient is elderly.
- Offer the use of essential oils and herbs if you believe it to be helpful in the recuperative process. If you have an understanding of the benefits of the oils and herbs that apply to a particular situation, blend your own mixtures or buy what is needed for the patient. Present it in a nice gift box, bag, or basket with an uplifting note and/or positive quote.
- Offer to get some shopping done for the family. This could include groceries, household goods, school clothes, or other items for the children.
- Be a chauffeur for the children if the parent or parents are recuperating from illness or surgery.
- Be aware of housecleaning chores that need to be done. Consider hiring a professional housecleaning service if there are funds available, or ask

for willing volunteers to help you. Such needs may be expected once a week for a couple of months or only a week or two.

- Gain permission to do outside yard work if it needs attention. Enlist teenagers in the neighborhood to help with this task.
- Attend to any house maintenance that is needed. Ask pointed questions about repair work. Get it done quickly.
- Bring a delicious chocolate treat for the patient and family, along with a humorous movie to watch when the time is right.

Suicide

It is said that the family of the suicide victim often feels some degree of guilt after the suicide. The feeling of culpability greatly increases their personal suffering and anguish. Those who want to help can feel stymied about what to do, how and when to help, and what is appropriate for this sensitive period of time.

There are many articles available which will help you know how to comfort or help the family of the suicide victim. These sources are useful in gaining a clearer understanding of the family's emotional agony. It will increase your own understanding and ability to better comfort and serve them. Other ideas follow:

- Contact 911. This alerts the authorities, police, and paramedics to begin the necessary paperwork that needs to be filed.

- Take charge of cleaning the area where the death occurred. Do your best to erase any physical signs of what happened.
- Contact the local clergy with which the family has a relationship. If there is no such relationship, ask the family if they would like you to get someone that you trust to provide this assistance.
- Contact immediate family members. Assist them in any way if you perceive a need.
- Provide food. Though on the initial day little thought will be given to eating, nourishment will help to sustain the family's strength for the tasks that need to be done. See page 37, "Let's talk food!"
- See the "Funeral" category for other suggestions that might be appropriate for this situation.
- Encourage the survivors to write a letter to the loved one that took his or her life. This will help them release the feelings they may not have had the chance to express. Hanging on to guilt, confusion, or anger is not healthy for their own spirits. They need an outlet for expression. A letter could be a positive step toward their emotional healing.
- Be sensitive to offhand comments such as "I would rather kill myself," or "I would die if I had to do that," or "take a flying leap." These trite phrases can be said flippantly with little thought to their impact if said in the company of one who has experienced the suicide of a loved one.

- Never say anything like:
    - "Oh no, not your brother! I had no idea he was that messed up!"
    - "How did he take his life?"
    - "Did you find him?"
    - "What did he look like?"
    - "Was there anything you did to drive him to it?"
- Bring a mouth-watering chocolate treat when things have calmed down a bit. Don't forget a warm, uplifting movie. (This is a time and case sensitive suggestion, but it may help.)

Unemployment (Touchy Subject)

When one loses his or her job through downsizing, layoffs, firing, or a territory or factory closing, it feels as though the world has collapsed. The continuity of paying the monthly expenses and obligations is gone. It is a stunning shock, a little like being adrift in the ocean with no shore in sight. One's sense of self-reliance, independence, and even self-worth plummets. A sense of insecurity rules supreme until the person has worked through the shock of not having a job.

Every unemployed individual has his or her time of emotional as well as physical (when the next job begins) recovery from this loss. Often one feels life has lost its direction. There is definitely loss of a sense of power and of feeling able to be in control of one's circumstances. Most people need some time to make the adjustment.

Some people may look at this as an opportunity for new adventures. Others can feel their life has come to an abrupt end. Until there is a change of attitude, or a change of employment status, it can be uncomfortable to visit or offer help. In the meantime, the following ideas may help them regain a feeling of control and faith that there is light at the end of the unemployment tunnel:

- Present them with a "Job-loss Survival Kit." The kit may include any of the following: movies, oversized sunglasses, or a great book to read. Suggest they take time to lounge in the backyard, or indulge in the time they have to watch their favorite movies. Keep it light, entertaining and amusing.

- Offer support. Listen. Let the person vent. Refer to chapter five.

- Drop off treats and/or meals anonymously.

- Discuss with them the possible benefit of a new resume. If you are proficient and know what you are doing, offer to help them; if you are not, find and suggest an appropriate resource and support.

- Avoid saying anything respecting material assets, such as, "Oh don't worry, look at the diamond ring you are wearing!" or "Look at the beautiful cars you are driving!" or "What are you worried about, you have a great house in which to live." Comments such as these are hurtful. These possessions do not reflect the dire, financial needs of the family.

- Consider sending flowers or a plant with a note attached. In the note offer encouraging words. Also consider sending money. Any amount is helpful, whether it is five dollars or fifty! (This could be done anonymously.) The need is great!

- Offer to accompany the head or heads of the family on that first journey to collect welfare food, if the family is at that point of need. Such support and love may be very much appreciated at that difficult time.
- Consider purchasing a few sacks full of groceries and anonymously leaving them on their front door step. Make sure to drop it off when you know someone is at home and will retrieve the food promptly. A "disguised" and anonymous phone call would be helpful! Dogs or weather damage would be a waste and a disappointment to the family.
- Inform them of any job leads of which you become aware. Use the contacts you have and network for them if it is appropriate and possible.
- When it is appropriate, bring them a tasty chocolate treat and share a warm, humorous movie with them!

Wedding/Reception

Though my children are not yet of marrying age, I have many friends who have experienced the stress and strain of preparing for a wedding and reception. From an outsider's point of view, the list of things to do seems unbelievably long and tedious, yet it is just that attention to details that make the event so rewarding and memorable. As I have gingerly offered my help on occasion, I have been amply rewarded with great appreciation from my worn-out friends. These suggestions are from veterans of this happy time.

- Come with a specific offer to help. This will give you control over what you would like to be in charge of. It will be very much appreciated.
- Take food to the family the day before the wedding. Be sure it is nourishing, strengthening and healthy. It will help keep their energy up for the seemingly endless list of things to accomplish.
- Share your wedding props and extra supplies with others to help keep their expenses down.
- Offer kitchen help during the reception.
- Offer clean up help after the reception. Not many people stay for this part of the fun.
- Offer your home to your friend's out of town friends and family.
- Just show up and say "I'm available."
- Go to the reception as an invited guest. This is a tender time for families, especially for the parents of the bride and groom, and they want you to share in their happiness while celebrating their child's joy.
- Get a card container for those cards that come without a present. This helps to prevent a loss. If you are in charge of the gift table, make sure the cards are taped to the present they come with which prevents the "lost card disaster." When the reception is over, take the gifts to the appropriate location for the bride and groom to open at their disposal.

- If the wedding ceremony is a private occasion, offer to help tend small children of relatives during the ceremony.
- If the ceremony is performed in a private residence, consider taking a home video if there is no professional photographer.
- Tending the children of out of town guests is appreciated when an activity for the family is adult only.
- Celebrate the success of a party well thrown with a delicious chocolate treat and a great, humorous movie on a night other than the reception!

Widow/Widower

I have been told that the experience of losing one's mate rocks a person to their core. Next to losing a child or a parent, I imagine the loss of a spouse is most wrenching. Refer to chapter four to gain some clarity and basic understanding of the grieving process. Individuals, suddenly shocked into awareness that they are now without their spouse, are often unable to think logically or practically. Should you come to their door ready to help, but without a specific task in mind, they may likely be unable or unwilling to give out assignments. Try to come prepared with a specific act of kindness in mind. Assess obvious needs and attempt to think of something beyond those that would be helpful. Then go to them and say, "This is what I would like to do." If they are not receptive now, leave graciously, and try again later. Here are some specific suggestions:

- Acknowledge the death of the spouse. Ignoring the impact of and the fact of the beloved's death is unsympathetic, unkind, and cold. Several widows emphasized this sentiment.
- Keep the acknowledgement short and sincere— "I'm sorry for your loss."
- Be sensitive to the cycle of healing. If you have a comfortable relationship with this person, call during the depression stage (weeks or even months later) and offer your love, encouragement, and a listening ear.
- Be careful not to let the person feel like the local charity project, especially soon after the loss. It creates a sense of finality they are not ready to embrace.
- Food is always helpful. Suggest that they consider eating at a different table than the one they shared with their spouse, if they have a choice.
- Very tactfully, suggest they consider the purchase of a different bed, and that smaller may work better. This suggestion is conditional on how close your relationship is and if there are means available.
- Offer to take this friend to social situations. Now single, he or she may feel awkward when there are other couples at these settings. They are more comfortable with friends and enjoying comfortable companionship. In their minds and hearts, they are still processing the emotional adjustment and acceptance of being a single person.

Do Something! Specific Ideas for Specific Situations 153

- Money is very helpful. Insurance money may take several months or longer to reach the family. Meanwhile, immediate expenses accumulate.
- Take your newly single friend on a date. Go out for a milk shake, a walk, or a short drive. Evenings are particularly difficult and lonely.
- Let your friend talk. Listen! Refer to chapter five.
- Plant a couple of pots with bright colored annuals while they are at the funeral. Keep the pots replanted each year on the anniversary of the death.
- Never say, "Just wait, it gets worse." (I know it seems obvious, but one woman was given this cold and insensitive comment shortly after her husband died!)
- Engage a crew of people to help you organize, prepare the soil, and plant the seeds of a vegetable garden for one who is used to having a garden. Make sure your friend has the energy to maintain the garden. If not, be prepared to maintain the garden as needed, or find willing individuals who want to help with this service.
- Hugs are always appreciated.
- If the widow/widower is a young parent, often what is missed most are the date nights away from the children when the adults can talk. Present him or her with an opportunity for a date and allow all the time needed to discuss important issues and brag about what the children are doing. Allow your friend to laugh and cry as needed.

- Keep in touch on a regular basis. Send notes and/or cards of encouragement, make regular, uplifting phone calls, or send them cheerful emails.

- Set up a weekly lunch date, either in or out of your home. If the friend does not feel like venturing out yet, bring lunch in once a week. The connection with a friend and the consistency of the appointment is very important. This activity is something to look forward to, as well as momentarily being a distraction from the painful loss.

- Remember birthdays and holidays with a call and a cheerful card.

- Try to time your calls at lonely times of the days and weeks, usually during the evenings and weekends.

- Be in charge of picking up donated food and returning the containers to the owners, or organize a schedule of volunteers to deliver meals as needed. Encourage the volunteers to use disposable containers when possible.

- Record the names of the people who donated flowers, either at the home, church, or funeral home. Specify what kind of floral arrangement was given. This service makes it easier to recognize the contribution with messages of appreciation after the services.

The following are suggestions for keeping in touch on a regular basis through a monthly luncheon. This may include one or more widows. It is ideal if you can find a group of women who like each other's company and enjoy the time spent together.

- o Have the luncheon on the same day of each month, for example, every third Monday. A set day and time works best. The women know what activity to plan for and when it will take place.
- o Pick up each woman and take her to the gathering place.
- o Allow enough time during and after lunch for visiting.
- o Serve "girl" food for a fun time. Take precautions and consider if there are food allergies.
- o Call ahead to remind your guests of the date and time.

- Don't neglect to try a yummy chocolate delight, followed by a warm, humorous movie every now and then! If it were a gentleman you are befriending, perhaps a warm pie and war movie would be more appropriate. Of course, humorous movies are great tonics for anyone!

Chapter 8

Putting the "Gentle" back in the Man

When I was twenty-six, I had the good fortune to work with Max. He was my boss and his motto was "this is how your job is done; this is how I like things run." During this learning curve of understanding my responsibilities, I was also taught with much firmness ("and there will be no discussing it, Terri,") that Max expected to familiarize me in the ways of gentlemanly behavior toward a woman by his example.

Growing up in the '60s & '70s, I learned the philosophy of feminism and was schooled in the inequality between men and women regarding a number of issues. These topics were regular headlines along with civil rights, Woodstock, and the Vietnam War. During this time of social and philosophical upheaval, some of the previous generations' ways of thinking were appropriately discarded. These included such issues as "children should be seen and not heard," or families never discussing skeletons in the closets. Equality issues between men and women such as workplace benefits, wages, and the right to work outside of the home, were also brought to the table. There were myriad points of debate on numerous subjects that caused people to question the way things had always been done.

I believe that my generation, in this era of free and open thinking, introduced a more informal approach to societal interactions between the sexes. There also seemed to be a movement toward increased familiarity between the generations. There were fewer children addressing their elders as "Mr." or "Mrs. Smith." There was noticeably less politeness with and respect for authority figures.

The attitude of free love and the antiestablishment mentality reigned supreme. Woodstock was one of those "wow" experiences. Some of the music presented was terrific. However, it was a place of opportunity for my generation to set aside conventional rules of behavior. Many people displayed such casual, even reckless, interaction with one another in public as had not ever before been witnessed. This lax attitude persists today.

These social voices were persistent and loud. The constant current of these attitudes permeated my education and shaped my psyche. At the same time, I did not live at an economic level that required Emily Post behavior. I was blithely clueless that for hundreds and hundreds of years, men actually deferred to women in the social graces! It was behavior reserved for the movies, not real life.

Then I met Max. He introduced me to the idea that it is noble and in good taste for men to defer to women in simple and thoughtful ways. He wasn't trumpeting his thoughtfulness to garner attention to himself. He wasn't trying to make some political statement. He was simply applying graciousness and respect for women that his generation had learned. I asked him who his role model was. He said there was no one particular role model. There didn't have to be. The whole of society acted this way. Everywhere men of breeding deferred to women. It was not done as a subservient gesture. It was done out of respect and societal mores.

I recall one day that Max and I were on an errand. As we were walking to his car, he reminded me not to touch the door handle. He said he would open the car door for me, as he had many times before. Between the office door (which he opened for me) and the car door, we were engaged in conversation. Out of habit and an "I can do for myself" attitude, I forgot his reminder and began opening my own door, with Max standing close behind. The door was immediately pushed closed. I received a firm, but loving scolding by my fatherly boss. "Didn't I just tell you not to touch the door handle?" "Yes, you did." "Well let me open your door. That is what a gentleman does."

Max considers it an honor to defer to women of all ages and persuasions of feminism. He is undeterred by ruffled feathers of womanly independence. He grew up in the '30s and '40s when courteous behavior to women was the generally accepted fashion. His belief is that we should allow men to be gentlemen.

Unless you live in circles where Emily Post and Miss Manners' philosophies are required behavior from the cradle to the grave, the generations of children from the '60s to our current time have not been exposed to regular, everyday, common courtesies displayed from men to women. Nor are women taught to graciously expect and receive it.

There seems to be a lack of awareness about manners between the sexes. If a man extends a kindness to a woman, such as holding a door open for her, it is often rebuffed, indicating the attitude of "I am capable of opening my own door." Or it is interpreted as being too familiar, with sexual overtones attached. The man can be left confused and offended himself. A look of rejection and a cold response from a woman will simply teach and reinforce men that the common courtesies offered are unwanted. This results in fewer attempts at politeness, and a quandary about roles of behavior and exactly what manners are appropriate between the sexes.

Of course, there are always men who are exceptions to the general rule I am implying here. There are men who have developed this sensitivity and consistently behave in a mannerly way to all women. Many women are also comfortable with expecting this quality of behavior from men.

It is my attempt to reassure that common courtesies between the sexes are a gift of self to give as a man and to accept as a woman. I offer the following list of suggestions to aid in raising our awareness of "nicety necessities." These can easily be taught and put into one's lifestyle.

As a gentleman, be aware of the opportunities to be courteous to women. There are many chances in your day-to-day activities to take advantage of displaying gentlemanly manners. Determine to make it a part of who you are. As a woman, allow men to treat you with respect by letting them act on their inclination to be gentlemen. Resist the urge to judge, to be indifferent, or to misinterpret their actions. It is permissible (and ennobling) to allow these courtesies to become a natural part of our interactions.

Civil, courteous behavior between the sexes is the focus here. Of course there are inappropriate, offensive, intrusive, and even criminal behaviors, which should not be tolerated. However, in our haste to make sure nothing untoward or offensive is even implied, we have allowed proper etiquette to be diminished. Our children need to model and experience proper manners. This creates a feeling of civility in them, which, in turn will contribute to an elevation of general goodness, and kindness in the world.

With practice, these kindnesses and courtesies can turn into habit. You will begin to be more comfortable giving and receiving them. These courtesies will bring out the higher and better characteristics of our beings. They will increase the refinement of our natures. The kindness and manners extended to men and women will help reduce the unfortunate competition that exists between the sexes. Men, try any of these recommendations:

- Open any and all doors—a car, the house, the workplace, a restaurant, the hospital, etc.
- Help a woman put on her coat or sweater as well as help her to remove it.
- It is a rare thing to see a man tipping his hat to a woman these days, simply because the only hats men wear are baseball hats. I doubt very much if they will be tipping their baseball hats any time soon. However, some of the older generation still wear hats occasionally and you may see them tipping or even doffing their hat to a lady. It's a nice gesture of respect that will soon slip into a societal custom of yesteryear.
- Retrieve a grocery cart for a woman if you happen to be in the shopping cart area. Wal-Mart gives customers a nice service. Many of their male door greeters offer shopping carts to customers entering the store.

- Be aware of automobile needs. Changing tires is a big deal to a woman. Tires are heavy, dirty and, let's admit it, a big fingernail breaker! Some women know how to change a tire, but the reality of it is that the task is difficult if you are not dressed appropriately, have children needing attention, or haven't adequate strength.

Some months ago, after playing tennis, I returned to my truck at the gym parking lot to discover that my back tire was flat! I know how to change a tire, but I simply don't have the muscle to get the lug nuts loose, lift the heavy tire off, and put on the spare tire. I went back inside the gym to recruit a young "stud" to help with the tire task. His boss, a woman, was hard to persuade. The young man pleaded my case. I overheard her say to him, "I don't pay you to help change tires." He was persistent, reassuring her it would only take him ten minutes. She allowed him to help me, but wasn't very happy about it. Of course, I was very grateful for his help. He did indeed accomplish the task in about ten to fifteen minutes.

Shortly after that incident, I did not see him working there anymore. It was a sad reminder of how cold our society can be! I have since thanked the manager for his help, but I believe it was too late to help save this young man's job.

- Hold the chair for the woman as she is seating herself in meetings, the restaurant, and other public places.
- Allow her to enter the aisle of the movie theater first while choosing a location to sit. (Hopefully she'll be sensitive to where the gentleman likes to sit.)

- Wait for her after leaving a social situation. Don't walk ahead of her. Escorting her as an equal is respectful and gentlemanly.
- While descending or ascending stairs, gently steady her by holding her hand or elbow if there is enough room.
- Let her take your arm when escorting her to functions.
- Offer to get her a refreshment or beverage.
- When in traffic, under crowded conditions, allow the woman to pull in front of you. It really isn't a competition. No one has to be in front of the pack. A little civility amidst all the road rage helps to reduce tension and anger between strangers. Of course, this holds true for women to be gracious to men also.
- Because men are built with more muscle mass than women, be aware of appropriate physical tasks that may need a man's helping hand. Some situations, activities, or tasks are too heavy or difficult for a woman to handle. For example, one day Max was working at his commercial building during renovation and he happened to be watching a woman attempting to back up her car. She would "rev" the engine, but nothing happened. She tried doing this several times. As Max became more curious about why the car was going nowhere, despite enough engine power, he noticed her front tires were lodged over the cement guard. Obviously, she did not have the

physical strength to lift her car off the guard. Max called a couple of other men over to offer assistance and the recruited team of "gentlemen" took care of her problem in a couple of minutes.

- Men like chocolate too! Warm their hearts with a great chocolate treat and a guy movie that would satisfy their interests.

These are a few suggestions that may help men and women begin to implement graciousness in their behavior toward one another. Initially, it may be uncomfortable. However, if allowed and practiced, it will do a lot to restore a man's masculinity and a woman's softness. Thoughtful and considerate interactions will promote gentility and refinement in humankind. It will bring gentleness to the core of our lives. Go ahead, give it a try!

Chapter 9

From Local to Global

This book has attempted to offer enlightenment regarding simple acts of kindness and gifts from the heart on a one-to-one basis. However, during the research of this project I became familiar with women who represent another facet of serving others. I realized I needed to bring attention to their efforts because the work they are doing has such impact. It has permanently changed their own lives as well as the volunteers who work within the organizations they have built. The communities that their projects target are profoundly affected for good by their efforts and are given hope for a brighter future. It would be difficult to judge which group of people are affected and transformed the most.

The women of whom I write are women like you and me. Each of them has taken a simple idea and combined it with determination, creativity, and passion. This has resulted in developing an organization that effectively nurtures relationships, heals hearts, and mends lives. They wanted to make a difference on a larger scale. I know there are perhaps hundreds or thousands of women just like these three individuals who have moved forward with a yearning to impact and change lives around the world. These examples might give one woman the courage and motivation to act on her desire to make a similar impact. I highlight these selfless women as great examples of what one person can do.

Perhaps you are an individual who would like to create a nonprofit group that focuses on service outside of your local community. You may connect with these women's vision and missions. Their stories are inspirational. They have impressive ambition and passion, which propels them to accomplish their goals. They are ordinary individuals bringing about extraordinary change. These women are Kathy Headlee, founder of Mothers Without Borders; Diana Tacey, founder of ChildLight Foundation for Afghan Children; and Judy Zone, founder of YouthLINC. I introduce them to you with honor. Here are their stories.

Kathy Headlee, Mothers Without Borders

Nurturing and caring for orphaned and vulnerable children as if they were our own.
—*Kathy*

I met Kathy two years ago at a gathering for women. She gave a brief overview of her organization with the emphasis on current projects. I was impressed with her vision and dedication. I hadn't seen her since, but as I was organizing the chapters for this book, I knew that I needed to include her story and I knew where I wanted her story to fit. I was fortunate enough to secure an interview with her in spite of her hectic schedule.

From Local to Global

Kathy came from a background where she was taught the importance of serving beyond self and giving to the community. She raised her five children with the same awareness and selfless principles. In 1990, she and her family were living in San Diego where access to Tijuana, Mexico is relatively easy. She drove her children to the orphanages in Tijuana and would engage in small projects, such as bringing toys and clothes for the children, or playing with them. During this same time period, she would also volunteer her time and services in helping battered women and the homeless in her local community.

Once her children were in school, she volunteered to work with a large humanitarian organization. From nine to three each day, she would learn the minutiae that makes a charitable organization function, such as stuffing envelopes, entering data into computers, answering telephones, understanding project development, fundraising, and staffing.

After several months, she was asked to take on a leadership role in some of the projects of the humanitarian organization. This leadership role fine-tuned her education in volunteer work. It allowed her to sharpen her ability to organize and pursue projects from start to finish. Kathy's confidence grew as she proved her capability and understanding of the inner workings of the organization. As a result, she was asked to sit on the board of directors, a position she held for ten years.

During this time of what Kathy calls "her training period," she was watching a program on Romanian orphans which, "pierced her soul." The content of the show spoke to her, and she knew she wanted and needed to do something. Just what that particular something was she didn't have a clue. Eight or nine months passed when a flash of inspiration helped her understand what that something was.

At a family reunion during the summer of 1991, a family counsel was held in which a suggestion was made that every other year the adults take a trip somewhere *sans* children. Kathy knew instinctively that Romania was to be the first destination of the all-adult trip. She also knew that it didn't have the same appeal as Hawaii, and that a Romanian service trip might be a "hard sell." Eventually everyone who would be able to go came to accept and understand that this choice was the right one.

In the spring of 1992, Kathy and twenty-two family members embarked on their "Family Reunion Service Project." They flew to Romania to assist the medical staff that had also volunteered their time, skills, and means. These magnificent medical specialists had been directed to an orphanage in Romania to correct such physical malformations as cleft palates, and clubfeet, in order to help the children become more eligible for adoption. Kathy and her family were also directed there to offer preoperative and postoperative services for these children.

After two and a half weeks of this labor of love, Kathy and her family members were changed for life. They returned to the United States exhausted from the difficulties of serving in a foreign country, but with a much keener awareness of how much each person had to offer. Not only did she understand that she had been preparing for just this kind of experience, but also that she would be blessed with the addition of a Romanian child to her personal family! Her brother's family adopted three Romanian children! Their lives were dramatically altered forever.

When word got out about the success of their trip, other family groups asked Kathy to help them organize and execute service trips of their own. This occurred several times a year, giving her an opportunity to fine-tune the process of overseas projects and expanding her volunteer work to other areas of need, such as Bolivia and Mexico. She also continued to educate herself in humanitarian efforts by attending helpful conferences.

During the mid 1990s, Kathy was narrowing her focus toward orphans. Much of her work seemed to naturally flow to these motherless and fatherless children. Parallel to this focus, she became increasingly aware of peculiar dynamics in two groups of people. First, she realized that the orphan population in the world exploded with the AIDS epidemic becoming pandemic. Second, she noticed that a sector of Americans was getting wealthier much younger. Many of these newly rich people wanted to contribute to the world's needs in ways that would make a difference. It became evident to her that these two groups were a perfect fit, as long as there was an avenue to funnel the funds so that they directly benefited the children in need. Her question then was, "How do I pull these two groups together?"

Drawing from her rich background and experience, she launched the nonprofit organization Mothers Without Borders, organizing projects in Romania, Bolivia, and India, and then centering the organization's efforts in Zambia in the year 2000. Kathy says there are four points of interest that Mothers Without Borders emphasizes. First, the organization works with local charities to identify children in need. Her Zambian staff is trained and prepared to receive containers of relief supplies that are distributed directly to the orphans.

Second, Mothers Without Borders goes into Zambian villages to assess the children's needs and evaluate the resources of the village to provide for the children. There is a determination of what is lacking in ways of goods and services. Mothers Without Borders steps in to fill the gap between these two evaluation snapshots.

Third, there is an emphasis and development of American volunteers. Their passion, expertise, and help are crucial to the success of this organization. Teams of twenty volunteers travel several times a year to work on their assigned projects in the countries where MWB is currently working.

And lastly, Kathy has a current project, called the Children's Village. MWB recently purchased fifty-five acres of land in Zambia, which will be the site of the first Children's Village. Here the organization will build homes for the orphans that are headed by a husband/wife team. This will give the children a family environment in which to grow and develop a sense of security and confidence. They will be allowed to live in the village until they reach adulthood. They will be strongly encouraged to participate in the village's success in whatever way they can. There will be a trade school for the use of local people to get an education in particular vocations that strengthen the infrastructure of the local community. Kathy's vision is broad, covering such fields as tailoring, brick making, poultry and pig farming, agriculture, gardening, health and hygiene education, HIV education, simple construction, developing a service club, and teaching basic interpersonal skills of cooperation.

There are overwhelming numbers of orphans and children in need in Zambia. As Mothers Without Borders continues to extend their arms of love to these children, their influence and support will aid in stemming the tide of rampant disease and ignorant behavior. The children whose lives they touch have hope for a future that has some measure of success. What the children do with this opportunity and gift that Mothers Without Borders offers them is, of course, their choice.

Kathy feels that by contributing her part to the ongoing vision of this organization, she is bestowing more goodness in the world, which elevates that cumulative effect of all the goodness that is offered by people worldwide. It is a positive, joyful message! Below is her contact information:

Mothers Without Borders

www.motherswithoutborders.org

mail@motherswithoutborders.org

Office phone: 801-796-5535

125 E. Main St. Suite 402

American Fork, UT 84003

Diana Tacey,
Childlight Foundation For Afghan Children

Diana has been a friend of mine since we were eleven years old. She moved to Oregon from southern California, complete with white lipstick, long, straight hair, and tanned skin. She represented the epitome of "cool" from my young perspective. I was completely enthralled with how she approached life in her relaxed, California way. I observed her over the years, happily entertaining our friends throughout high school or becoming very concerned about and involved in the current social issues of the times.

When I made a phone call to her several years ago to get caught up with each other's lives, I was not surprised to learn that her catering company was flourishing. She had built it from a desire to entertain and a love of cooking, which talents she now shared with the Mesa, Arizona community. What I was surprised to find out was that in addition to this very full time job, she had started a nonprofit organization to help the women and children of Afghanistan. This is her story.

Not long after the terrible events of September 11, 2001, Diana began paying closer attention to the reviews, articles, and reports about Afghanistan. In December 2001, she read an article on the Internet by Kathy Gannon, Islamabad Bureau Chief for the Associated Press. It was called Kabul's Forgotten Orphans Suffer. Kathy was the only western journalist in Kabul at the time the US bombing occurred and forced the Taliban to flee. The article showed a photo of a little boy at an orphanage looking out of the window. The article had a powerful effect on Diana and she felt drawn to these children and this part of the world in a way she could not fully explain. Diana contacted Kathy expressing her desire to do something. She was directed to contact individuals that were very familiar with the situation in Afghanistan. A meeting and phone call with one person led to more contacts and phone calls, until in April 2002 she contacted a woman who suggested that if she was serious about making an impact she should work with the Abdul Haq Foundation, a nongovernmental organization (NGO) based in Afghanistan. Abdul Haq was this woman's brother who had been instrumental in repelling the Russian invasion in Afghanistan and had earned the respect of world leaders, such as Ronald Regan and Margaret Thatcher, as well as local Afghan freedom fighters. Abdul was betrayed at some point while attempting to enlist support from his tribal brothers to side with US and western allies against the Taliban and Al Qaeda. He and a nephew were assassinated the day after they were caught and arrested.

In April of 2002, Diana contacted the director of the Abdul Haq Foundation who was the brother of the late Abdul Haq. He appreciated her interest and desire to help. His first e-mail to her began with, "Thank you for trusting us." He invited her to visit, and said he would personally arrange for accommodations and care in Jalalabad and Kabul. He would also introduce her to some of the teachers and principals at some of the schools that needed help and she could decide for herself where she wanted to work and what she wanted to do.

She chose to call her new organization "ChildLight Foundation for Afghan Children." Diana liked the imagery that children are full of light and that their eyes sparkle with sweetness, hope, and love. She was also inspired by the famous words of William Wordsworth:

> **Our birth is but a sleep and a forgetting:**
> **The Soul that rises with us, our life's Star,**
> **Hath had elsewhere its setting,**
> **And cometh from afar:**
> **Not in entire forgetfulness,**
> **And not in utter nakedness,**
> **But trailing clouds of glory do we come**
> **From God, who is our home:**
> **Heaven lies about us in our infancy!**[1]

---

1. William Wordsworth, "Ode: Intimations of Immortality from Recollections of Early Childhood," in *Selected Poems and Prefaces by William Wordsworth,* ed. Jack Stillinger (Boston: Houghton Mifflin, 1965), 186-191.

After securing $12,000 from a fundraiser (that her company catered), she was able to take her first trip to Afghanistan in July 2002. Her father and another male acquaintance went with her as escorts because of the very male dominated, patriarchal society in which she was going to be traveling. During this first trip, she was introduced to the culture, foods, attitudes, beauty, and desperate needs of the area.

She was escorted from Peshawar, Pakistan, through the Khyber Pass, and finally to Jalalabad. Diana was introduced to several possible projects that caught her attention. As her involvement with these people's needs became more extensive, her awareness of other pockets of needs expanded. ChildLight Foundation has since focused on the following projects to improve the lives of the children and people in Afghanistan.

- A school for orphan girls in Jalalabad has been improved by the donation of a variety of school books. The Foundation has arranged for an art workshop to be introduced and conducted at the school. ChildLight Foundation provided art books, pastel chalk, watercolor and oil paints, and other supplies. This developed into a request for an enclosed art and computer room which is a current project that will include desks, chairs, computers, a printer, a world map and a chalkboard.
- A small village about forty-five miles from Jalalabad called Hesarak had an outdoor tent for a school that housed six hundred and fifty children with very little supplies, no well, and no medical facilities. Over the past four years,

ChildLight Foundation has provided six new tents, has dug a well to provide clean drinking water at the school site, and has built a 1200-square-foot school building. The school now contains classrooms and a health-worker office with a desk, a bookcase, books, chairs, and basic medical supplies. The foundation supplements the salary of the female health worker who is also a teacher at the school.

- Diana met the Director of a western Kabul school called "Karte Se Day School." This school is well run and operated by the NGO "Children in Crisis of London." Diana's organization supplements their lunchtime feeding program with vegetables, fruit, and occasional beef and chicken.

- Diana sponsored a fundraiser in Tucson, Arizona that provided four computers and two printers for a new computer lab at the Nangarhar Medical School in Jalalabad. This medical school trains eight hundred students and ChildLight Foundation's contributions became the first computers provided for the students. They have also sent *Physician Continuing Medical Education* CDs, workbooks, and a complete set of medical textbooks that were requested from the school on a wide range of medical specialties.

- ChildLight Foundation has developed a boys' youth soccer program at the Jalalabad Boys Orphanage. Equipment and uniforms for two teams were designed and sent with the assistance of a member of the rotary club of Peshawar, Pakistan.

- Diana has since joined Rotary International and her local rotary club is working in conjunction with ChildLight Foundation to develop four female-operated Poultry Farms in Jalalabad, all operated by single mothers and widows with the support and assistance of their children and families.
- They are currently working on raising funds of $44,000 for construction of a new Jalalabad Public Library.

ChildLight Foundation continues to move forward with their focus on small projects that bring big changes in the lives of the people they help. It is Diana's hope that ChildLight Foundation will be able to help meet some of the needs of the children in the corner of Afghanistan where they are working. She desires to facilitate and encourage greater peace and understanding between our two cultures.

After her annual trip to Afghanistan in September of 2004, she was talking with Sarah, one of her team members. She is an Afghan American woman who speaks fluent Pashto and was originally from Kandahar. Sarah related a conversation she had with one of the young girls during an art workshop at the Fatima Zehra Girls Orphan School. The young girl had asked Sarah if all Americans were like Diana. Sarah asked her, "What do you mean? Blonde-haired and fair-skinned?" "No," she said, "Kind and respectful of our culture and customs."

Diana had no idea she had made this kind of an impression. She felt happy and satisfied that there were a few girls who knew first hand that there were Americans who were kind and cared about them and treated them with respect. No matter what any one else might say about Americans, this young girl would be able to speak up and give a good word for Americans as she has come to know from her personal experience and the influence that ChildLight Foundation has had on her young life. Diana's contact information is below:

ChildLight Foundation

www.childlightfoundation.org

email: taceyinmesa@msn.com

Phone: (480) 964-5484

1959 S. Power Road

Suites 103-245

Mesa, AZ 85206

Judy Zone, YouthLINC

Open the cage and let something fly in.

—*Judy*

It began with Sara, Judy's daughter. For many years, Judy put money away on a monthly basis for Sara to spend as she wanted when she turned eighteen. Judy thought Sara would spend it on college tuition or on a new car. When the time came for Sara to decide what to do with the funds, she surprised her mother with the suggestion that they go on a safari!

Judy and Sara found themselves in an eclectic mix of people in Kenya, including their male guide and a group of women who simply didn't speak to each other. They were hungry for information and knowledge about the local people and their conditions. The guide educated them about the areas in which they would travel. With this information and exposure to an area that obviously needed assistance, Judy came home with the genesis of a plan.

Judy had recently dropped out of a doctoral program and had returned to the public education arena where she had taught secondary school for twenty years. She was left with a space in her life that allowed her to consider what she wanted to do next. Judy witnessed the impact of the safari on her daughter. Sara had put together in her mind the local needs, the international needs, and how horrible it was to live in an underdeveloped country where the civilians had no safety net, no local soup kitchen, no medical clinics, and where the people were starving. These conditions Sara assimilated and understood. Judy clearly saw the impact this trip had on Sara and the character growth that had occurred.

After her Safari with Sara, Judy had some months during the summer in which to consider the direction she wanted to take her desire to help and serve the people in Kenya. Being in education for so many years, she developed an appreciation for the potential for service and leadership that young people in America have, but usually don't tap into. She knew that if they were given the right informational tools, given the ability to develop leadership skills, and more importantly, given the opportunity to stretch themselves beyond their immediate gratifications, they could make a significant and positive difference in the lives of the people she had met in Kenya.

So YouthLINC was born. She proposed that young people earn sponsorship to offset the costs of expensive international trips through local service and education. She offered sixteen high school students an opportunity to serve in Kenya for a couple of weeks during the summer. She needed $25,000 to fund her first project. She became, as she calls it, a "street beggar." She literally went from business to business explaining her idea of service and the students' involvement. She contacted two hundred and fifty businesses, soliciting them to invest in the students' humanitarianism. Only one business did not donate funds to her. With expenses covered by the donations of these generous businesses, Judy was able to launch her first trip to Kenya in the summer of 2000.

However, this was not the common humanitarian concept of jump on board, fund your trip, and get placed into a service project already developed. Judy's goal was to shape the minds and attitudes of the students in a way that would positively alter the way they felt about helping other humans less fortunate than themselves.

She requires that the student who is interested in working with the YouthLINC organization be willing to give one hundred hours of community service. This works out to be about three or four hours a week from the beginning of the school year until the following summer, prior to going abroad. Also, the student volunteers are required to attend monthly meetings. At these meetings, volunteer mentors and team leaders explain the goals of the project for each site. These leaders then allow the young people to come up with a working plan for collecting the necessary items that will be taken to the site during the summer. If there is a need for a certain amount of medical supplies, the volunteer figures out how to collect what is needed.

Also, the student volunteers are coached in the skills and knowledge needed for the project. For example, in the tiny village of Yanamono on the Amazon River in Peru, the people were in desperate need of dental care. A group of YouthLINC students learned how to take dental histories and teach dental hygiene, so that when the American dentist arrived, the intake exams were already done.

Another need was teaching the young people in Mexico that smoking cigarettes is harmful to their health. The YL volunteers assigned to this project spent time learning information about the short and long-term effects of smoking. When they went to Mexico, they were put to work educating the local young people with the information they had gained. This is in addition to the one hundred hours of community service work that they do during the year.

The current projects are focusing on three sites: Kenya, Peru, and Mexico. There are approximately twenty to twenty-five youth assigned per site. There are several mentors and team leaders that organize and oversee each site. Judy coordinates the details to ensure that no trips overlap. Once the trip to Kenya is completed, Peru will be launched, and when that trip is finished, the trip to Mexico begins.

YouthLINC's aim is to initiate and inspire the young American into the path of service, beginning with service at the local level. If you are interested, contact Judy at:

youthlinc@xmission.com
www.youthlinc.org
Phone (801) 467-4417
Fax (801) 467-1982
1140 E. Brickyard Rd. #71
Salt Lake City, UT 84106

Chapter 10

"Mankind Is My Business"

In the classic story, *A Christmas Carol*, Ebenezer Scrooge is visited and instructed by his old, dead business partner, Jacob Marley. Ebenezer is introduced to the concept that there must be life outside of one's self. While Scrooge tries to comprehend the specter and his message that are before his eyes, Marley is desperately striving to convey to Scrooge the importance of serving one's fellow man.

'Oh! Captive, bound, and double-ironed,' cried the phantom, 'not to know that any Christian spirit working kindly in its little sphere, whatever it may be, will find its mortal life too short for its vast means of usefulness… Not to know that no space of regret can make amends for one life's opportunities misused! Yet such was I! Oh! Such was I!'

'But you were always a good man of business, Jacob,' faltered Scrooge, who now began to apply this to himself.

'Business!' cried the Ghost, wringing its hands again. 'Mankind was my business. The common welfare was my business; charity, mercy, forbearance, and benevolence were all my business. The dealings of my trade were but a drop of water in the comprehensive ocean of my business!'[1]

So Scrooge is given an opportunity for a lifestyle change. This change embraces a chance and hope of escaping Marley's fate of roaming the afterlife fettered in chains. These, he explains, are chains he forged in life "link by link and yard by yard." Scrooge is compelled to view his past, present, and future by three spirits who illuminate and educate his narrow view of mankind. After a night of looking honestly at the results of a life lived from a small, mean, and selfish heart, Scrooge cries for mercy from the last spirit as he is shown his final fate of a cold, forgotten grave with "EBENEZER SCROOGE" engraved on the face of the stone.

'Spirit!' he cried, tight clutching at its robe, 'hear me! I am not the man I was. I will not be the man I must have been but for this intercourse . . . The Spirits of all three shall strive within me. I will not shut out the lessons that they teach. Oh, tell me I may sponge away the writing on this stone!'[2]

In his desperate agony of soul, he collapses on the top of his future grave, thinking all is lost for him, only to find himself in his own bedroom, with "all Time before him (as) his own to make amends in!"

---

1. Charles Dickens, *A Christmas Carol* (New York: Gramercy Books, 1982), 243.
2. Ibid. 581

"Scrooge was better than his word. He became as good a friend, as good a master, and as good a man, as the good old city knew, or any other good old city, town, or borough, in the good old world. Some people laughed to see the alteration in him, but he let them laugh, and little heeded them; for he was wise enough to know that nothing ever happened on this globe, for good, at which some people did not have their fill of laughter in the outset; and knowing that such as these would be blind any way, he thought it quite as well that they should wrinkle up their eyes in grins, as have the malady in less attractive forms. His own heart laughed: and that was quite enough for him."[3]

Although Ebenezer Scrooge is a fictional character, he represents a good portion of human beings that haven't made the transformation from selfish to selfless. It is inspirational to witness this change in a person. There are thousands of true stories the world over, from culture to culture, that recount examples of uplifting acts of compassion that have buoyed the spirits of the downhearted. Many publications such as *Readers Digest, Guideposts,* and a myriad of Internet Web sites are dedicated to printing positive, warm-hearted and edifying stories of people serving and helping each other. Exposure to these accounts contributes to restoring our faith in the basic goodness of people.

There is rampant negativity and heartbreak in this world of ours. Television, magazines, and newspapers convey, ad nauseam, the ugly side of human nature. We are continuously exposed to the disasters that bombard and disrupt our

---
3. Ibid. 585

communities, the deceptions of many of our politicians, and the unrealistic and immoral standard of living that Hollywood too often portrays.

This constant exposure to so much negativity subtly affects the attitude we have toward ourselves, the manner in which we approach each day's activities, and how we interact with those who cross our path. It leads to heaviness in our souls. This heaviness manifests itself in attitudes that are bleak, pessimistic, and unenthusiastic. From this unattractive emotional place, the activities and interactions we create result in less than fulfilling exchanges for everyone.

Being surrounded by such negative energy gradually seeps into our souls, which in turn depletes our stores of positivism, causing a fear-based mentality. This fear then triggers in us a suspicion of other peoples' agendas and motives, which feeds our negativity. We develop a genuine lack of interest in anything except our own agendas. We are suspect as to what will be taken from us. So we hoard our time, means, and talents, fearing we could be taken advantage of only to promote someone else's plans. This state of fear and negativity then feeds into the negative energy of a family unit, creating a sense of futility and hopelessness. The hopelessness filters back into the communities as we go about our business, the negativity then permeates the world, and the cycle perpetuates itself.

Interjecting acts of kindness and serving others into this unhealthy cycle of negative energy, attitude, and selfishness, is the antidote to the poison that, if left unchecked, rapidly spreads from person to person. One simple act of kindness and love to another human being lifts the spirits of the giver and receiver, contributes to a healthier emotional environment, and spreads hope for a better world. Think about it. If you anonymously picked up the tab of the person behind you at a tollbooth, or at Starbucks, or a movie theater, you will have spread kindness and surprise, which generates a feeling of pleasure. It may not remain long term with the person, but at some level inside they can't help but be grateful for the anonymous generosity. They may even pass this selfless principle along in their own way.

These positive gestures and acts aid in dispelling fear, despair, and a feeling of hopelessness for the giver and the receiver. If nourished consistently, this refreshing feeling of hope and comfort turns into satisfaction, relief, and gratitude. Nurturing these sensibilities creates a desire to pass along, to someone else this same gratifying sensation of goodness. This then inspires more acts of kindness. And the cycle perpetuates itself.

I would encourage each of us to learn from the lessons that Scrooge was taught. We would do well to make mankind more of our business in our "busyness." As we engage in good works and charitable acts, we will enlarge our souls while we create and distribute light in a world that is overrun with darkness.

Conclusion

The person who invests the most time studying, researching, and teaching a subject always gains the most out of the experience. So it has been for me. I have benefited immensely from the information I have gathered regarding acts of kindness and serving others. I have gleaned tremendous insight into the absolute need to develop a servant's heart. Learning precise ways to move myself out of my own comfort zone to lift a fellow human being has been of incalculable benefit to my inner character. I have been enlightened with the knowledge that to extend oneself to others in spiritual and emotional life-saving actions saves one's own spiritual and emotional life.

I have been humbled by the inspiring acts of love and aid that so many anonymous contributors have shared with me and allowed me to make public. I have been inspired to be courageous. Go and make a difference in someone's life, big or small! It doesn't matter what it is, just do it! No matter how one's act of service may be received, the real measure of merit and value is the intention behind it. With a clear intention, a pure heart, and focused purpose, your follow-through to serve will reap rewards for your personal growth. You will immediately benefit by increasing your own feeling of self-respect and gratitude!

With this new clarity, I have carved out more space in my soul for deeper compassion. I have allowed margins in my day for the possibility to help another. My attitude for availability has completely changed from "if I can fit it in" to striving to cultivate situations where I can contribute. As one expresses one's love through action, he or she creates greater room and capacity to love. This in turn feeds a desire to love and serve again. The more you live this plan of action, the more you want to serve. The more you serve, the more you love, and the more you love, the more you serve.

When I had my first child, nothing consumed me as much as the love I felt for him. It was overwhelming to receive such a gift of deep love for another human being. I was unprepared for the abundance and breadth of this new quality of love. It was idyllic, magical, and satisfying. When I was expecting my second child, I was fearful that I would not have the same amount of love for him as I had for my first child. I fretted, worried, and assumed that I lacked the capacity to love two children equally. After my second baby was born, I immediately realized and felt my capacity to love both of these children with the same fierce love, for that love had doubled. When I was expecting my third child, I knew I had plenty of love for her and any other children that would come into my family.

So it is with service and extending acts of kindness. When you offer yourself in this way to another human being, you enlarge your capacity to perpetuate these kind acts. But the hidden gift that I did not expect was the desire to continue to offer kindnesses and service. It is a contagious yearning. You double and triple your capacity and desire to give. With each offering, your soul expands, increasing your ability to be "the pencil in God's hand," as Mother Teresa referred to herself and her work. We, too, can be an effective "pencil."

I have come to appreciate the quality of being joyful. This

is an inherent state of being. To discover inner joy is to discover one's own true nature. To nourish and sustain that joy is to know how to serve others. Maintaining that joy is the reason to get out of bed in the morning.

While putting into action some of the ideas in this book, I have lived a richer life in the last year. Initially, I took baby steps because I was so unused to interjecting myself into strangers' lives. I am now much more comfortable with volunteering my hands, my time, and my talents.

I have learned to allow for the magic of stillness. It enhances the healing process as you listen to another's heartache. Stillness is the place where you hear whisperings. These whisperings give guidance and wisdom beyond yourself. The stillness is the lush foundation of the soul, where a quiet, random, and gentle thought can take root and flourish. It is in the stillness that answers come to mend broken hearts. It is in the stillness that we learn the how to help when we have no clue as to where to begin. It is in the stillness that we are taught divine lessons. There is definitely magic in stillness.

I have come to appreciate the value of giving and receiving—they are delicately balanced partners in the cycles of life. They are intertwined to teach us all the dignity of serving with compassion and receiving with grace. Both have equal merit. Both have equal value. There cannot be one without the other, or there is no gift.

I have learned more deeply about gratitude. Of course I am grateful for all those who have contributed their wisdom, their creative ideas, and their life experiences. Without their insight and willingness to share their knowledge, the heart of this book would not have come together. Words cannot express my thankfulness for the lessons learned. I am a different woman because of this journey, a difference for which I am profoundly grateful.

The challenge now is to apply this information that has been assembled. We are accountable for having grown in particular knowledge of what we can do. We cannot use the excuse, "Well, I just don't know what to do." It will be a measure of our characters as to how we use this information from today forward.

I encourage you to have the courage to step outside of yourself and begin or continue to spread—far and wide—aid, assistance, and love. As you begin each day, make the effort to connect with your higher and better self to increase your awareness of someone's cry for help. Be available in spirit in order to be useful in body.

It is a good possibility that you will never know the full benefit of the contribution you will make in someone's life, or maybe you will have a very good idea of the value of your charity. Either way, you have lifted two souls, theirs and yours. You are, in fact, not Mother Teresa. Nor would you want to be because you have your own unique gifts that will be a salve and tonic for those people you are helping and loving. However, you can emulate her simple desire to "love one, one, one." You can be better than you are. Just do your best and when you do, you will make a difference!

Joy must be one of the pivots of our life. It is the token of a generous personality. Sometimes it is also a mantle that clothes a life of sacrifice and self-giving. A person who has this gift often reaches high summits. He or she is like a sun in a community. If you are joyful, it will shine in your eyes and in your look, in your conversation and in your countenance. You will not be able to hide it because joy overflows.

—Mother Teresa[1]

---

1. Edited by Carol Kelly-Gangi, *Mother Teresa, Her Essential Wisdom,* (New York: Barnes & Noble Publishing, Inc., 2006) 72, 73

A Note about References

Throughout this book I have made reference to several sources that would be of help in a specific category. I had anticipated drafting a list of sources that would be useful to the readers and including them in the back of this book. However, as I began the process of gathering this information, the task became overwhelming and daunting. There were literally 435,000,000 web sites listed when I was searching for "support groups." There is so much help available, starting with the Internet as a resource, that I could not do this reference section justice. I feel each source needs to be scrutinized and determined useful by the person doing the searching. So I surrender finishing this arduous task of gathering this information and my attempt to be fair and inclusive.

I would encourage each reader to seek out the support group or networks that would be useful for him or her in their individual situations. During my attempt at gathering this information, I realized there are amazing, talented, and willing people who want to help. The Internet is the easiest, most convenient place to begin looking for help. Local libraries are also a great source for local resources. Federal, state, and local agencies are listed in the front of community telephone books of many government run resources which can be very useful.

There is much value in a person getting in touch with and involved to some degree with a support group or network of loving and helpful individuals. I would encourage those readers who feel a need for more support and information for their individual situations to find resources and people that will help them feel emotionally safe, understood, and progress on their personal path towards healing and wholeness.

Biography

Terri Cannavo graduated cum laude with a Bachelor of Science degree in family science. She has spent the last twenty years developing a working knowledge of her degree by raising three terrific children. While supporting her husband as he developed his career and maintaining a pulse on the family busyness, her interest in learning, understanding, and promoting a woman's individual potential increased exponentially as her children demanded less of her time.

Eventually, she developed a complete curriculum to teach and guide women to discover their personal, unlimited potential. After teaching this information for over a year, she was persuaded that writing her first book would be a more effective way to get her message out to a greater number of women. Besides authoring this current publication, Terri is also the host of the Internet radio show *Skid in Sideways* on www.grapevineradio.com. The show focuses on celebrating the joyful-girl aspect of a woman's personality. Terri is dedicated to bringing a sense of hope to women who want more from themselves and who know that with this personal improvement, they will elevate the level of goodness in the world around them.